MUSTANG

Anniversary edition 1964-1994

FORD

MUSTANG

MUSTANG

Anniversary edition 1964-1994

Nicky Wright

MMB

This edition published in the United Kingdom in 1994 by MMB,
an imprint of Multimedia Books Limited,
32/34 Gordon House Road, London NW5 1LP

Exclusive distribution in the USA by
Smithmark Publishers Inc.
16 East 32nd Street, New York, NY 10016

Copyright © Multimedia Books Ltd 1986, 1994

Editor: Maggi McCormick
Production: Hugh Allan
Design: Kelly Flynn

A catalogue record for this book is available from the British Library.

ISBN 1 85375 167 7

Printed in Spain by Cayfosa, Barcelona

Dedication
**For Becky. A woman of very special
merit whom I love very much.**

**A very special thank you to Tom and Karen for
being such wonderful friends.**

CONTENTS

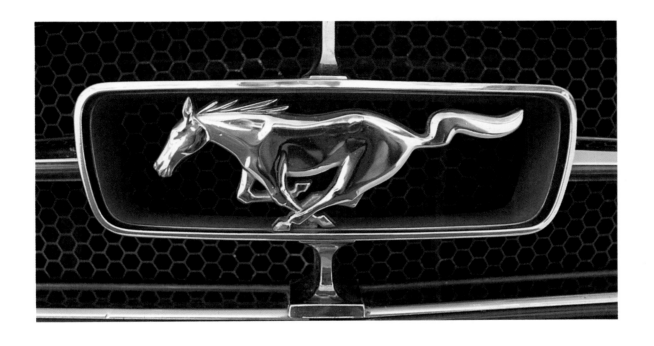

At rest this '68 Shelby GT350 looks
mild enough, but it's tough enough to
take on the very best.

INTRODUCTION

I t doesn't happen often, but it happened on Friday, April 17, 1964. A truck driver, mesmerized by the sight of a new car gleaming bright in a San Francisco showroom window, drove straight through it in a complete trance. The reason for the truck driver's unorthodox entrance was Ford's latest creation, unveiled to the public for the first time that warm spring day. Compact and unashamedly youthful in appeal, the Mustang had arrived. A brilliant and expensive media campaign had heralded the car's arrival, and a public fully prepared greeted the Mustang with sentiments approaching the hysterical. That was the reason for the truck driver's enthusiasm. It doesn't happen often, but Friday, April 17, 1964, turned out to be one of the most extraordinary days in the annals of motoring folklore.

Today the Mustang, particularly those models built between 1964 and 1973, is treated with respect around the world. It has become surrounded with a legendary status every bit as grand as Ferrari's or Lamborghini's or the other great marques. Enthusiasts of over-priced Italian exotica might shudder to think that their pride and joy shares a podium with a brash little upstart stamped out in hundreds of thousands in factories from Dearborn to L.A. That's only natural. The Mustang, though, was no elitist automobile; it was built to a price, and corners were cut to give everyone the chance to own a sharp-looking, youthful and sporty car.

A happy car, an honest car, the Mustang succeeded beyond even the wildest dreams of its creators. This is its story.

Basking in the sun, this '68 Shelby GT-500 is a real handful if roused.

BIRTH OF A LEGEND

It is 1960, the dawn of a new decade. The two-term Eisenhower presidency was drawing to a close, and Democratic hopes were riding on a handsome, youthful senator called John F. Kennedy. From an American point of view, life looked pretty good, the barometer set fair to the distant horizon. Vietnam was just another name in the school atlas; the violent maelstrom was yet to make itself known. The Sixties had begun and the good times were here to stay, right?

Things also looked pretty optimistic in what was left of one of the greatest contributors to America's wealth. The motor industry had prospered mightily over the previous 15 years, though deaths in the family of such great names as Packard, Hudson, Nash and Kaiser had occurred through lack of foresight and misguided attempts to follow the Big Three in doing what the Big Three knew best. Not that the giants escaped entirely: 1960 would see the end of De Soto, as well as the industry's biggest debacle, the unloved Edsel. Instead, three new marques were born, not as replacements for those that had perished, but as a result of a ground swell of new thinking affecting the land.

Falcon, Valiant, Corvair, these cars of the new age were truly newcomers in more than just years. The belief that bigger is better had taken a tumble as the public began buying smaller, more fuel-efficient cars from Europe. American Motors – the outcome of the 1954 Hudson-Nash merger – gauged this changing trend and reacted first with the Rambler, which in 1959 occupied eighth place in the overall sales charts. Ailing Studebaker rushed out its cleverly reworked, down-sized regular car and christened it the Lark. The enterprising independents had created a new approach, and the public was sold.

Not that they had it their own way for long. As previously mentioned, GM, Ford and Chrysler, backed by enormous resources and talent, took no time to launch their offerings. Of the three, Chevrolet's Corvair was the most radical, with its air-cooled flat six at the rear and independent suspension all around. Ford's Falcon was as conventional as the Corvair was radical, while the Valiant arguably had the prettiest styling of the three. As it was, the conservative Falcon outsold the other two by a wide margin—almost twice as many as the technically advanced Corvair. That the Falcon was so successful reflected the fickle tastes of the consumer. The stylistic flamboyance of the Fifties simply wasn't popular any more. If any one group or company was responsible for this change of fashion, it was Ford under McNamara.

FAR LEFT AND LEFT. *Two decades separate these cars. Though unrecognisable from its record selling 1964$\frac{1}{2}$ forebear, the 1984 Mustang GT–350 convertible proudly carries on the tradition set by its illustrious ancestor.*

Had former Ford president, Robert McNamara (above left), not left to serve in the Kennedy administration, the Mustang might never have been. It was the new order, headed by McNamara's successor Lee Iacocca (above right) that changed Ford's direction from plodder to performance.

McNAMARA'S NEW DIRECTION

McNamara, who replaced Lewis D. Crusoe as Ford Division general manager in 1955, was strictly a dollars-and-cents man. His enthusiasm for cars was confined to whether they would make money or not. No longer would Ford build unprofitable cars with the excuse that they were a nice idea at the time. Under McNamara's direction, the change in policy was absolute. All cars Ford Division built would be designed purely to make a profit.

Fortunately for today's collectors, McNamara took over too late to stop the unique Ford Skyliner retractable hardtop from going into production, as well as the beautiful 1955 two-seat Thunderbird, which was already in the showrooms. Not that either car was safe from cancellation. Skyliner sales amounted to only 49,394 over three years, while the classic T-Bird managed a little over 43,000 before McNamara gave them both the ax. Style was out as McNamara's conservative anonymity presaged the demise of the elaborate "art deco on wheels" school of design.

It is only fair to point out that McNamara wasn't entirely responsible for the four-seater Thunderbird that made its debut in 1958. Factions in the Ford hierarchy had never been too sure of the wisdom of producing a sporty two-seater. Henry Ford II, however, was, and who was going to argue with the chairman of the company? He wanted to eclipse Chevrolet's Corvette with a more stylish, luxury-oriented boulevard cruiser with sporty pretensions.

Not only did the 1955 T-Bird eclipse the Corvette – it

totally dominated it. First-year sales amounted to 16,155 Thunderbirds against Corvette's 674! Much of the car's success can be attributed to the then Ford Division general manager, Lewis B. Crusoe. He wanted nothing too outrageous or macho, but a car that would appeal to everybody, men and women alike. It would have flair, a V8 engine as standard, and would be marketed as a "personal car."

The result was arguably the prettiest car to appear since the end of World War II, its beautiful styling being largely the work of two Ford designers, Robert Maguire and Damon Woods. These two gave the car strong product identity – wrap-around windshield, peaked headlight farings, round taillights – but avoided the use of chrome ornamentation and two-tone color schemes. Maguire and Woods put simplicity back into the automobile and in doing so created a classic.

No matter how spectacular the Thunderbird looked, there were still those in Ford's Dearborn headquarters who were not convinced. Crusoe had been moved up the company ladder, his position filled by Robert McNamara. Now the doubters had their way; almost as soon as the 1955 T-Bird hit the showrooms, work began to develop a four-seat model for 1958 aimed at the luxury end of the market.

At as little as $3,000, the two-seater 1955-57 Thunderbird sold reasonably, if not spectacularly, well. Over three seasons 53,166 were produced, but it was not enough for McNamara, who refused the suggestion that it should continue in production as a companion model to the luxury four-seat car. That McNamara's faith in the new unit-bodied T-Bird was justified goes without saying – nearly 40,000 were built in what amounted to a depression year for the industry, but his decision to cancel the original two-seater was both hasty and shortsighted. Fortunately for sportscar enthusiasts, GM's Chevrolet division proved more loyal to its slow-selling fiberglass-bodied Corvette. There had been talk of axing it, but common sense prevailed.

So the car the original Thunderbird had been designed to challenge became firmly entrenched, not only as America's only sports car, but eventually as a car able to equal or better Europe's finest sporting automobiles. Ford would have to wait six years before it had a worthy contender, and even then it was no contender for the Mustang, which as we shall see, wasn't designed to take on the Corvette. Not in its standard form, anyway.

Iacocca was ably assisted by Ford design chief, Gene Bordinat (left), the man responsible for Mustang's overall styling. It was the design team of Joe Oros (above) whose Mustang II prototype was finally selected as the basis for the eventual production car.

Ford got cold feet over what is arguably the world's most beautiful postwar automobile. The 1955-57 two-seat Thunderbird didn't sell enough to satisfy the corporate accounts department and was axed in favor of a larger, four-seater luxury "personal" car. However, its size and style played a part in evolving the Mustang. Shown here is a 1956 model.

A DULL-TO-DEMON DECADE

As America entered the Sixties, 1959's exuberant mobile excesses gave way to McNamara-style conservatism. With one or two exceptions, the 1963 Riviera and Corvette Stingray being cases in point, Detroit's standard offerings were bland, nothing-to-write-home-about cars. Efficient, yes. Memorable, no. Then a few inventive folks started dropping big engines under the conservative hoods and began a whole new game. Chevy 409s and Ford 500/XLs started what was to become one of the most extraordinary eras in motoring history. Short-lived the muscle cars may have been, but their effect was profound. What started out as "brute force and ignorance" in the late Sixties rapidly gave way to sophisticated handling, or as sophisticated as it could be, bearing in mind those cars' limited scope; clever engineering innovations and performance capable of taking on – and beating – most of Europe's ultra-expensive exotica in a straight line. If not always on a sharp right-hander.

While the Sixties started out as rather dull, they ended in a blaze of wildcat, tape-striped performance glory. It was also the age of another unique manifestation from the auto-designers' drawing boards. This was the pony car, and in any mention of pony cars it is the Mustang that immediately comes to mind.

Had Robert McNamara not gone on to higher things (he became Secretary of Defense in the Kennedy Administration, then president of the World Bank), the Mustang might never have been. In fact, it wouldn't have taken root, nor would Ford's Total Performance Program have gotten off the ground, and the likelihood of Ford winning Le Mans would have been as remote as a successful Edsel! Certainly McNamara left Ford in a healthy financial position, but one wonders how long this would have been the case had he remained. Drab cars equate with monotonous food: both might be good for you, but the human spirit soon requires a bit of excitement to rekindle its appetite. Henry Ford II might not think so, but his choice of Lee Iacocca as general manager of Ford Division was perhaps the most astute decision he ever made. It certainly resulted in a period of innovation and excitement the company needed after McNamara.

Before looking into the various decisions that resulted in the Mustang, let us take a look at the context in which those decisions were made, beginning with the fabulous, flamboyant Fifties. For possibly more than at any other period in the automobile's development, it was during this decade that the stylists were given their head. Not that car design in the sense of artistic expression was anything new; just look at what was built during the Thirties. Coachbuilders proliferated and a customer could ask for any body style that took his fancy. This was all very well, but not everybody could afford to own a personalized Duesenberg or Packard. What about the blue-collar work-

RIGHT. If you wanted cars that moved around corners with alacrity, you went to Europe. But if sheer artistry on wheels was your thing, the American car of the Fifties was the way to go. Harley Earl, the doyen of automotive styling, was responsible for beauties such as this 1950 Cadillac 60S hardtop.

Gordon Buehrig's beautiful Cord is universally recognized as a work of art. This one is a 1937 supercharged 812 convertible currently resident at the Auburn-Cord-Duesenberg Museum, Indiana. Ahead of its time, the Cord exemplified the idea of the automobile as "rolling sculpture."

ABOVE. *From any angle, Buick's 1953 Golden Anniversary Skylark looks right. If nothing else, it represents an era when the automobile was at its peak in terms of artistic expression.*

er who wanted a little styling on his mundane $500 runabout? Alfred Sloan came to his rescue and set a precedent that the Mustang would keep alive for three decades to come.

Sloan was a man of vision. As early as 1921, he had dreamed of a car that by its very looks would be enough to make a would-be purchaser's heart beat faster with desire of ownership. It was Sloan who, as head of General Motors, set up the first design studio for the sole purpose of making the mass-market automobile as desirable as the custom-built cars produced by Murphy, Brunn, Dietrich, and the like. To this end, in 1927, he set up GM's Art and Color Department under the direction of Harley Earl.

We don't need to elaborate about Harley Earl; suffice to say his artistic genius changed the world of motoring forever. He was responsible for GM car design from 1927 until his retirement in 1959. His creations are works of pure art and shall always remain so. Another great artist of the same kind is Gordon Buehrig. His 1935-37 Cord 810/812 series is arguably the finest design ever to ride on four wheels. No wonder it has been acclaimed a work of art by the New York Metropolitan Museum of Modern Art!

CHROME VISIONS AND "ROLLING SCULPTURE"

If the styling of the Thirties can be recognized as art, surely too can those chrome visions of the Fifties. Here was, as the title of Gordon Buehrig's book suggests, "rolling sculpture." It didn't matter whether the car was cheap or expensive; they all looked bright, right, each one shameless in its invitation to take you to the stars.

The names behind these automobiles are legion. Harley Earl; Gordon Buehrig, who played no small part in the design of the 1956 Continental Mk II; the genius of Virgil Exner whose Mopar first launched Chrysler on its comeback trail; Raymond Loewy, whose chief designer, Robert E. Bourke, was responsible for the stunning 1953 Studebaker; Eugene Gregorie of Ford; Richard Teague; Howard "Dutch" Darrin. These were the men whose work has become part of this century's culture. Without doubt the years 1953 through 1957 produced the finest examples of postwar design. Cast an eye over a 1953 Buick Skylark, a 1955 Chevy Bel-Air or Nomad, a 1957 Chrysler. In this age of decals and plastic, one marvels at the attention given to interior trim. Heavily chromed, sculpted door handles, for instance, or steering wheel hubs; each item a fine detail to be admired. As for the badges, ornaments and exterior-script, the same quality is readily apparent. Look at Cadillac's shield, or Chevrolet's: intricate patterns crafted in bas-relief, plated chrome and gold; a kaleidoscope of colors delicately applied between the crowns and lions, stars and crests. Admire other sophisticated touches like the gas filler hidden behind Cadillac's taillight; the little "gun sights" atop a Dodge; Ford or Chrysler front fenders, designed to serve as parking aids. They don't build cars like this any more.

What the critics of these cars – and they certainly had their detractors – failed to recognize was the climate into which these cars were created. The Fifties were boom years for a United States still reasonably insulated from the rest of the world. Not affected by European cultural influence (of which there was very little in the Fifties anyway), America went its own way. Art and design belonged, not to class or university intellectuals, but to the people. American culture is mass culture; from its music to its cars, it is culture for the people, of the people, and owned by the people. Not always good, but better for it overall.

Nowadays, cars of the Fifties are rapidly becoming recognized for their artistic worth. "You look over a car like a '57 Chevy and you can't see a line out of place," one young man, not even born when that particular Chevy was current, remarked to the author. Ignored as being dowdy in its day, certain '57 Chevrolet convertibles have been known to command as much as $30,000. Several

other Fifties' cars change hands for handsome five-figure fees which show no sign of leveling off.

The critics were, however, right in one respect: handling and braking were definitely suspect in most of these cars. Some were so deficient in these areas as to be completely unsafe. The situation was compounded by the fact that most of the money went into styling and creating new designs every couple of years. It wasn't that the technology was absent; superb innovations like Chrysler's hemispherical V8, Chevy's 283, automatic transmissions, many firsts taken for granted today, either appeared or were perfected during the Fifties. Unsafe in inexperienced hands the Fifties, automobiles may have been, but as objets d'art they had no equal.

Through its music and its writers, its movies, architecture, cars, and even its soft drinks (Raymond Loewy also designed the Coca–Cola bottle), American populist culture led the way through the first half of this century, revolutionizing preconceived concepts that somehow art belonged to the few. Traditionalists scorned this brash new ideology founded apparently on bad taste. This taste, however, is purely a matter for the individual; if it pleases, then it's good. Today, American culture spans the globe. The American Dream is everybody's dream. Lee Iacocca may well have thought so when he dreamed up the Mustang. He lived through America's greatest period and no doubt assimilated much that he observed, whether consciously or not.

BELOW. The voluptuous look wasn't confined to GM, as this 1948 Chrysler Town & Country shows. Hand-finished ash and mahogany doors and trunk set this Chrysler apart as one of the world's first "personal luxury cars."

ABOVE. *Art on wheels was by no means confined to limited-production expensive automobiles, as this 1957 Chevrolet Bel-Air convertible demonstrates so well.*

IACOCCA'S AMERICAN DREAM

Lee Anthony Iacocca was born of Italian parentage. His parents' arrival in the New World was followed by hard work and eventual prosperity, all the ingredients of the American Dream.

Nicola Iacocca, Lee's father, came to America in 1902. He was only 12 when he arrived and he was alone, having left his native San Marco in southern Italy to seek his fortune in the new land that promised so much. He lived for a time with his stepbrother in Garrett, Pennsylvania, but shortly moved to Allentown where he had another brother. Working mainly as an apprentice shoemaker, Nicola saved enough money to return to Italy in 1921, with the express purpose of bringing his widowed mother back to America. While he was there, he met and fell in love with a seventeen-year-old girl named Antoinette. Shortly afterward, Nicola returned to America

with his new bride and his mother and set up home in Allentown. Three years later, on October 15, 1924, Lee Iacocca was born.

Shortly before Lee came into the world, his father had opened a hot-dog restaurant called the Orpheum Weiner House. It was a successful venture, successful enough for Nicola to bring Lee's uncles into the business. In fact, Lee's cousins still make hot dogs to this day, and there was a time Lee thought of going into the food business himself.

The success of the Orpheum and other enterprises prompted Iacocca Senior to go into the car rental business. So he bought into a national company called U-Drive-It. It wasn't long before Iacocca had a fleet of rental cars, about 30 in all, of which the majority were Fords. Young Iacocca soon developed an interest in the automobile and, with the encouragement of a friend in the auto-

retail business, decided that cars were to be his life.

At school Lee was an attentive pupil, graduating with excellent grades. His strength of character was already showing, his ability to deal with a major crisis given a serious test in 1939 when he was struck down for six months with rheumatic fever.

Like thousands of other patriotic young Americans, Lee tried to enlist at the outbreak of World War II. Because of his medical record, he was classed 4F. In his book *Iacocca, An Autobiography*, he says that he felt he was the only young American who wasn't out there fighting the enemy.

Convincing the Air Force he was fit was a wasted effort so Lee went back to his books. At the same time he decided to try for a scholarship in engineering and was accepted by Lehigh University which was only 30 minutes' drive from his home.

At Lehigh he studied hard for eight semesters, got a bachelor's degree, and thought about a job. Engineers were in short supply during the war, and anyone with Lee's abilities was naturally in great demand. Although he had the pick of some 20 job offers, Lee wanted to work for Ford, especially after being deeply impressed with a 1940 Lincoln Continental. Anybody who could build a car like that was worth working for! Out of several students interviewed by Ford at Lehigh, young Iacocca was the one chosen. He was over the moon, as well he might be. When school finished, he took a short break with his parents, and while vacationing, he got a letter from Lehigh's placement director, enclosing a flyer outlining an offer for a chance to go to Princeton. Lee called Ford, who told him to go for the chance; they would hold a job for him once he had graduated. Everything was coming up roses for Lee Iacocca.

ABOVE. Another Harley Earl creation was the 1954 Corvette, today recognized more for its style than its sporty attributes, which left much to be desired. Although it is now classed as one of the world's great sports cars, the current Corvette hasn't quite the panache of its ancestor.

IACOCCA: FROM DEARBORN TO DEALERSHIP

A little over a year later, a master's degree in mechanical engineering from Princeton in his pocket, Iacocca arrived in Dearborn, home of the great Ford Motor Company, to take up work as a student engineer. In essence it meant Iacocca was a trainee, part of a training program laid on for promising administration material. The course was designed to take young hopefuls through every stage of automobile manufacturing.

After nine months, from the foundry to final assembly, the supervisors sent Lee to the automatic transmission group. He still had nine months of the program to complete when he began to realize that he didn't want to do an engineering job for the rest of his life. He wanted, he said, to be "where the real action was." He wanted to go into marketing or sales.

The program supervisors were, understandably, disappointed. He would have to leave Dearborn and make his own way if he wanted to get a job with a Ford dealership. However, they gave him a letter of recommendation and wished him well. Lee was on his way back east

to try his luck with any dealership willing to listen.

After one or two false starts, Lee landed a post in the fleet sales department of a Ford dealership in Chester, Pennsylvania. By 1949 he was zone manager for his area and by 1953 assistant sales manager. All the while he was learning, learning. How to sell; how to deal with people; how to inspire confidence. Car selling, as he soon found out, is a rough, tough business. And it was especially so during the first postwar decade.

In 1956 Ford cars weren't selling as well as they might, and consumers gave Ford's pioneering safety program – dished steering wheels, dash padding and safety belts – the thumbs down. To help sales in his area, Lee instigated a time-payment plan he christened "56 for 56." What happened was this: for a 20 percent down payment, the customer would pay an affordable $56 a month over three years for a 1956 model.

To make sure his message got through, Lee Iacocca and other salesmen scoured local parking lots for late model cars, leaving a box of potato chips on the windshields of selected vehicles with a note which read "The chips are down. Wujatake $s for your car? We're selling

BELOW. Chrysler's family of cars scored some notable successes in 1957 with some of the most beautiful creations to come out of the Fifties. Styled by Virgil Exner, they became an inspiration for all others to follow, and follow Chrysler they did. Long and low, fleet of line, and with graceful soaring fins soon copied by everyone else, Chrysler's 1957 models could be likened to the Impressionist school of art. Perhaps the finest of all Chryslers was the 300C personal luxury muscle car. Powered by a 375 bhp hemi V8, the 300C was able to top 135 mph with ease. Common to all Chrysler products was torsion bar front suspension, which revolutionized Fifties' handling.

LEFT. Every day was a summer's day on the highways of the Fifties for cars like this 1955 Ford Fairlane Crown Victoria.

BELOW. Ford beat Chevrolet in sales for the first time in years with all-new styling in 1957. Shown is a 1957 Ford Fairlane two-door sedan, one of the cheaper offerings in the series. Even so, its good Thunderbird-inspired styling gives it an air of elegance belying its cost. (Wide whitewalls were the norm at the time; narrow whitewalls made their first appearance in 1962.)

'56 Fords for '56 a Month." Not sophisticated but Iacocca's plan was simple and direct. With no hardship to anyone, Iacocca's idea took off like wildfire, and soon the Philadelphia districts which were his responsibility became the top Ford sales area.

Good ideas don't take long to be noticed, and soon Iacocca's dramatic success was recognized in Dearborn. Robert S. McNamara, one of the financial whiz kids who had joined Ford in 1946 and who was now Ford Division's vice-president, was so struck by Iacocca's scheme that he made it part of Ford's marketing policy. For Iacocca, events now began to move very fast. He was given the position as district manager for Washington, D.C., as well as marrying May McLeary, a

ABOVE. *Straight up, canted or gull-wing, fins soared in every direction on America's 1959 cars. This 1959 Buick Electra 225 convertible, an attractive car with an elaborate grille made up of a series of rectangular chrome squares, favored the canted variety. Designers weren't afraid to try anything during the Fifties, costs appearing to be no object.*

receptionist he had met at the local Ford assembly plant in Chester. Just as the couple were preparing to move to Washington, Lee was summoned to Dearborn. The result of this momentous meeting was that, after ten years, Lee Iacocca was brought back to Ford headquarters as national truck marketing manager. A year later he became head of car marketing, and in 1960 he was given the responsibility for both.

On November 10, 1960, McNamara became president of the company and Lee was promoted to vice-president and general manager of the Ford Division. In the world outside Dearborn, John F. Kennedy narrowly defeated Richard M. Nixon to become the next President. A few days later, Kennedy offered McNamara the position of Secretary to the Treasury. McNamara declined but accepted Kennedy's next offer as Secretary of Defense.

McNamara's legacy to Ford had been the Falcon compact, introduced a year earlier. It sold tremendously well, partly because of its low price, which meant a low profit margin. Neither did it have a wide selection of options which were traditional money spinners. Looking at it, Lee formulated ideas for a car that would catch the public eye and make a handsome profit as well. The idea behind the Mustang was beginning to take shape.

IACOCCA TAKES CHARGE

Lee Iacocca had come a long way in 15 years. Here he was, at the age of 36, the general manager of Ford Division. Daunting as the job might have been, Iacocca characteristically rose to the challenge and took to it like a duck to water. Although he was a tough businessman, he liked cars and was determined to put Ford on the map with a world-beater. He was young enough to appreciate new ideas, yet experienced enough in the car business to put those ideas into practice. The current Ford line, though selling well, was dull. There was nothing for the ever-growing youth market to get excited about. And it was youth, so long neglected by Detroit, that Iacocca felt needed cultivating.

One of McNamara's final acts as head of the Ford Division was to authorize development of the Cardinal. This was a front-wheel-drive, V4-powered compact to be built in Germany. By the very nature of its size, performance and practical design, it was intended that the Cardinal would be an economical, no-frills car — just what the account books needed as far as McNamara was concerned. Now that Iacocca had taken McNamara's place, however, it was up to him to take overall responsibility for its development.

BELOW. One of the cars to be canceled during McNamara's reign was the splendidly opulent 1959 Ford Skyliner Retractable Hardtop. Only in the Fifties could such a car have taken root. But what a terrific idea, even if it was a shade impractical. Today this car is a highly desirable collector's item – what a conversation piece at the country club!

CARDINAL MISGIVINGS

Shortly after his promotion to head of Ford Division, Lee flew to Germany to evaluate the Cardinal. Straightaway he realized that this was not a car Americans would break records to buy. On his return he told Henry Ford II that the Cardinal was a non-starter for the American market. Ford's senior management and board of directors discussed Iacocca's misgivings, but it was his persuasive arguments that carried the day. The Cardinal was dropped, and Lee was free to pursue his beliefs in the market potential offered by America's youth.

Almost as soon as he took over as general manager, Iacocca began to inject a bit of life into Ford's premier stable. Too late to influence the 1961-62 models, he concentrated on mid-year 1963 offerings. The Galaxie was given a new, racy two-door model with a sharp fastback roof, while the Falcon finally got a V8. Called the Falcon Futura Sprint, its appeal represented the opposite of everything McNamara's policies had stood for.

Actually, the Sprint was the go-faster version of the hastily produced Falcon Futura coupe, built to take on Chevrolet's Corvair Monza, introduced at the end of the 1960 model year. It was initially designed as a trim option variation of the standard Corvair, with bucket seats, full carpeting and additional instruments. Up to the time of its announcement, Corvair was nowhere in sales compared to the Falcon. Even so, despite its late debut as a 1960 model, 12,000 Monzas were sold. In 1961 a four-speed gearbox was offered, no doubt helping gain the Monza nearly 143,000 customers. An even better year was 1962, when a convertible and a 150 bhp turbo-charged version were introduced. Sales for the Monza and Monza Spyder passed the 200,000 mark.

Of course, the Monza's success was recognized in the Ford camp, hence the Futura and and the sporty Futura Sprint which came as convertible or hardtop, replete with all the extras necessary to extol its performance image. Ford's sister division followed it with its Falcon-based

Comet, adding the S-22. Between them the Sprint and S-22 added 73,000 units to their respective division's compact lines in 1963, increasing to 118,000 in 1964.

In a way the Corvair Monza confirmed Iacocca's argument that there was a large market who wanted – and would buy – cars with pizzazz and youthful appeal. So in 1961 he started to develop his ideas with a group of bright young men from the Ford Division. Once a week, they would go for dinner at the Fairlane Inn in Dearborn. Here they were able to discuss freely, without constraints, various ideas of what sort of car they felt needed to be built. Because these meetings always took place at the Fairlane Inn, the group called themselves the Fairlane committee.

The committee consisted of Iacocca; Donald N. Frey, Iacocca's product manager; Hal Sperlich of product planning; marketing executive Frank Zimmerman; Walter Murphy, Ford PR manager; and Sidney Olson from Ford's advertising agency, J. Walter Thompson. All were in agreement with Lee's concept for a youth-oriented car,

especially as the public relations department was receiving a steadily increasing number of letters begging for the return of a car like the classic 1955-57 Thunderbird.

Public interest for a similar car to the Thunderbird – one of the loveliest designs ever to take to the road – convinced the Fairlane committee that either tastes were changing – because the original T-Bird only sold around 18,000 units a year – or, and more likely, the nation's youth wanted a sporty car. The committee agreed that the time was right to research public opinion more closely, and so Ford marketing manager Chase Morsey, Jr., launched a market research program to see whether Iacocca and the committee's hunches had some basis in fact. Meanwhile, the committee designated the project T-5 to give it some form of identity.

Morsey's research team went to work and came up with just the results the committee expected and hoped to hear. The survey's conclusions would have a marked effect, not only on Ford but on the whole industry's thinking throughout the Sixties.

Chevrolet's sporty Corvair Monza Spyder sold well enough to convince Ford to develop the Mustang. Besides influencing Ford's decision, the Corvair was the root of Ralph Nader's campaign for safer cars, resulting in direct Federal Government involvement from 1968 on.

RIGHT. Ford designers listening to Gene Bordinat (pointing) describing the design of the Mustang I (clay in foreground with modeler John Cecil). Far right stands the designer of the T-Bird, Bill Boyer.

BELOW RIGHT. Modelers (left to right), Arthur Rockal, Bonnie Flores and John Cecil shaping Mustang I clay.

ABOVE. Painters spray a fiberglass cast of Project T-5, the Mustang I. Clay models sometimes cracked before presentation, so Ford designers developed vinyl sheets painted the chosen color, which were spread on the model like wallpaper.

RIGHT MARKET, RIGHT TIME

To begin with, the survey found that the market was about to be flooded by millions of teenagers born during the postwar baby boom. They would reach car-buying age between 1960-65. Even more interesting was the fact that the population of young people between the ages of 15 to 29 would increase by 50 percent between 1960 and 1970, while the 30 to 39 age group would decline some nine percent during the same period. The researchers also discovered that this influx of youth would be better educated, more affluent, and possess far more ideas about the sort of cars they wanted to buy than the previous generation. Of the under-25s polled, 36 percent wanted bucket seats and four-speed manual transmissions, with economy of operation way down the list.

Another important point was the huge increase in two-car families. It was discovered that a second car was normally smaller and sportier than the main family automo-

bile. What is more, more single people were buying cars, and their choice was generally something more exotic. As Iacocca points out in his autobiography, this was a market in search of a car and not the other way around, as car makers, through force of habit, traditionally believed.

Once the Fairlane committee had sifted and analyzed the results of Morsey's research, a picture of the type of car they wanted began to emerge. It should be distinctive to look at and sporty to drive. It would not be a large car, more the size of the compacts of the day. Whether the car should go the whole sports car route and have two seats was still a matter for conjecture. One body of opinion believed that the new car should be a revival of the original two-seat Thunderbird, which was never actually classed as a sports car – not even by Ford who advertised it as a "personal car." Then there were those who thought it better to go for four seats in a sporty-looking package. Ideas flew back and forth with no definite deci-

ABOVE LEFT. Cob Briggs (left), public relations manager of Ford Engineering & Research, looks pensive while Engineer Herb Misch discusses the Mustang I clay with stylist Gene Bordinat (right).

LEFT. Don Frey (left), Ford Product Planning Manager and one of the Fairlane committee, looks over the Mustang I with Gene Bordinat.

sions being taken. The next step was to design and build a one-off prototype for critical assessment. This car, when it was built, was a brilliant study in advanced design, perpetrated by a trio who called their car the Mustang I, even though the overall project was still officially referred to as T-5.

MUSTANG I PROTOTYPE

Ford's Executive Stylist, Exterior, John Najjar, was chiefly responsible for the design of the Mustang I. He put together a package containing a full-size rendering and some drawings which he showed to Ford's Styling Vice-President, Gene Bordinat, and R.H.Maguire, Design Director. They were much impressed and showed the designs to to Herb Misch, who came to Dearborn via Studebaker-Packard. Misch was Ford's Vice-President of Engineering, and he, too, was taken with Najjar's concept which embodied a mid-engine configuration.

Hardly a year goes by without some motor manufacturer presenting a radical concept car for the edification of press and public. Quite often, these are non-running shells that are nice to look at, but not much else. Nobody wanted the Mustang I to be so fated; to make the media stand up and take notice required a fully operational car.

Roy Lunn was assigned by Misch to engineer Project T-5. An Englishman, Lunn came to Ford with an impressive list of credentials. His engineering background at Aston-Martin easily got him the job as Ford Engineering Manager at a time when the Number Two company was heavily into its Total Performance program. Obviously enthusiastic about the Mustang brief, Lunn tackled the job with aplomb. Considering the little time he had, Lunn performed miracles.

Styling for the car was done under the direction of Bordinat in Ford's advanced styling studios. The whole thing took just 21 days from the drawing board to clay

ABOVE. Only 40 inches high, the Mustang I was completed in time for its debut at the United States Grand Prix at Watkins Glen in October 1962. Painted in U.S. racing colors, the car featured a racing-style windshield. A stock windshield, "T" type roof, and rear and side glass had also been designed in case the car made it into production.

ABOVE. *A nice photograph taken by Ford Photographic of the rear of the Mustang 1. Although the trunk area looks capacious, there was no space under the lid, which covered the four-cylinder engine amidships.*

model, fast by anyone's standards. Aerodynamically sleek, with a wind-splitting frontal area similar to, but more refined than, Plymouth's 1970 Superbird, the Mustang I stood a mere 40 inches high, but possessed a ground clearance of five inches. A permanent roll bar was positioned behind the cockpit, and the headlights were retractable.

If Najjar's concept was an eye-opener, then Lunn and Misch's mechanical innovations would have left even Europe's most advanced technology in the shade. The engine, which was based on the ill-fated Cardinal's German-made power plant, was derived from Ford's Taunus 12/15 M but modified for use in the Mustang I. It was a 60-degree V4 with pushrod-operated overhead valves displacing 1,497cc and developing 109 bhp at 6,400 rpm. With a compression ratio of 11:1 and a bore and stroke of 3.54x2.32 inches, this oversquare unit boasted twin dual-throat Weber carburetors connected by a cross-over manifold. Another version, however, relied on a single-throat Solex, and in this guise the engine put out 89 bhp. Presumably, the smaller of the two was meant for road-going cars; the twin carb set-up was obviously aimed at competition had the car ever reached production.

In one of many departures from the traditional Detroit norm, the engine was mounted laterally behind the cockpit and cooled by two small radiators at each air inlet positioned ahead of the rear wheels – a quarter of a century ahead of one of Ferrari's latest models, the Testarossa! To each radiator were mounted thermostatically controlled electric fans which turned automatically

should the water temperature rise above the predetermined level.

In addition to these innovations, the car featured all-around suspension supplied by wishbones, splayed coil springs, and shock absorbers. At the rear, the suspension had upper wishbones similar to the front and lower triangulated arms connected to radius rods. Attachment points were widely spaced for good all-around distribution. Every spring and shock was adjustable for height and firmness. This suspension system was very advanced for its day and was much applauded by the world's motoring press, who recognized the extraordinary designing talents of Lunn and Misch.

Transmission for Mustang I was a four-speed transaxle with a cable-operated gear change. This unit was also derived from the Cardinal, but used a seven-and-a-half inch diameter clutch with special linings based upon the clutch used in the British Ford Consul. Also "borrowed" from the Consul were the disk/drum brakes, which had a dual master cylinder and were manufactured by Girling of England. Another British addition were the magnesium wheels shod in 5.20x13-inch tires supplied by Lotus. Rack and pinion steering developed for the Cardinal was used, but the steering links, outer ball joints, and steering arris came from the Consul. What was unique about the steering, however, was the column connected to the rack and pinion. A full eight inches of the column was flexible, thus allowing a decently raked steering wheel on an almost horizontal column. Steering ratio was 15:1, which gave a laudable 2.9 turns lock-to-lock and a turning circle of 30 feet.

BELOW RIGHT Executive stylist John Najjar (center, white shirt), meeting with stylists and engineers in the styling studios. Both Herb Misch and Gene Bordinat stand on his immediate right.

BELOW LEFT. Englishman Roy Lunn, formerly of Aston Martin, before joining Ford as a member of the Vehicles Concept Department, gazes thoughtfully at a design board with Herb Misch. Lunn and Misch were principals in the engineering of the Mustang I.

BODY INSPIRED BY NAJJAR

So, the mechanical side was pretty unusual, but what about the bodywork that all those goodies were clothed in? That, as we have mentioned before, was a masterpiece of overall design originally inspired by John Najjar. The outer skin panels were produced from stressed aluminum, .06-inch thick. The cockpit section, complete with non-adjustable seat (the steering column, however, could be moved three inches and the pedals were fixed to a sliding box member which also allowed adjustments), was integral with the body, as was the roll bar, thereby adding extra rigidity. Under the outer skin was a multi-tubular space-frame, each tube manufactured from steel and one inch in diameter. The aluminum panels were riveted to the frame, providing a design of enormous strength in a car that weighed only 1,148 pounds.

Because it was aimed at the MG/Triumph market, the car was small, even by the compact standards of the time. The height was 39.4 inches while its overall length was a mere 154.3 inches, sitting on a 90-inch wheelbase. The girth was a petite 60.8 inches. All in all, the Mustang I was quite a spectacular car and the most advanced vehicle to come out of Detroit in a long time.

As the Mustang I had to be completed in a hurry, Roy Lunn realized it would be impossible for Dearborn to build it in time. Misch also recognized the problems and called in outside help, the contract going to expert special car builders Troutman & Barnes of California. A full-size fiberglass cast to be used to form the outer aluminum body panels plus all interior/exterior ornamentation, taillight assemblies, exhaust and air intake grilles, instruments, interior materials, and blueprints were shipped to Troutman & Barnes' L.A. workshops. Working around the clock, Troutman & Barnes completed the car in record time: the Mustang I was ready to roll!

Amid much publicity, the Mustang I introduced itself in October 1962 to the crowds assembling at Watkins Glen to watch the United States Grand Prix. It was an ideal setting for Ford to show off the car because everybody who was interested would be there: the world's motoring press, racing personalities and sportscar enthusiasts, as well as the general public. When word got around that Ford was displaying an innovative prototype with a possible view to putting it into production, probably more interest was shown in the Mustang I than in the Grand Prix itself.

Dan Gurney drove the car a couple of laps around the Watkins Glen circuit. So did Stirling Moss. Both thought the car was sensational, and the motoring press thought so, too. *Car & Driver* road-tested the 89 bhp version shortly afterward and said the Mustang I reminded them of the first two-seater Coventry Climax-engined Cooper, but was actually better. The magazine heaped praise on the car's handling, cornering, braking and precise steering, though the editors had reservations about the lack of trunk space. The engine took up all the rear, and the front was loaded with spare tire, fuel tank and various hydraulic mechanisms. They came to the conclusion, though, that a few modifications would soon cure that problem.

Built the way it was, the Mustang I easily met FIA and SCCA regulations for sports and racing cars (suggesting that Lunn and company had an eye on future competition

ABOVE. An engineering design sketch of the Mustang I. The circle at the front of the car illustrates the recessed lighting arrangement.

LEFT. Two Mustang I models were built: one purely for show, the other as a running prototype. Here is the latter about to go through its paces.

LEFT. *Watkins Glen, October 7, 1962. Lee Iacocca invited star race driver Dan Gurney to try out the Mustang I. Gurney took it around the circuit a few times, driving the V4–powered car at speeds of 120 mph. Here, Gurney is seen talking to Roy Lunn on the day.*

BELOW. *The Mustang I in full flight at Watkins Glen.*

RIGHT. *Another view of the Mustang I taken at the end of the day. Although it was not put into commercial production, it showed the world what FoMoCo could do.*

BOTTOM, LEFT AND RIGHT. *The functional, well-designed interior, featuring full instrumentation, was put together in a matter of days by Ford's studio.*

activities). The engine could power the car to 115 mph and make the standing quarter in 18.2 seconds. And that was with the less potent of the engine options, as the British *Autocar* magazine found when its editors were given the chance to road test it when the car was shipped to Germany for evaluation.

Autocar's editors were impressed. They liked its gear change, which they considered "delightfully light yet precise," as well as the quick steering. They found the suspension gave a ride "as comfortable as any medium size sedan and fully able to cope with all kinds of road irregularities." But as everyone else had said, the shallow, racing-style windshield afforded little protection to a tall driver, and driving in the rain could create a bucketful of misery as there was no top. The designers said they proposed to modify and rectify these shortcomings.

TRIUMPH SHORT-LIVED

All said and done, the little Mustang I was an unqualified success. Lee Iacocca, however, was not impressed. He had carefully monitored public reaction and come to the conclusion that it was only a small group who were mak-

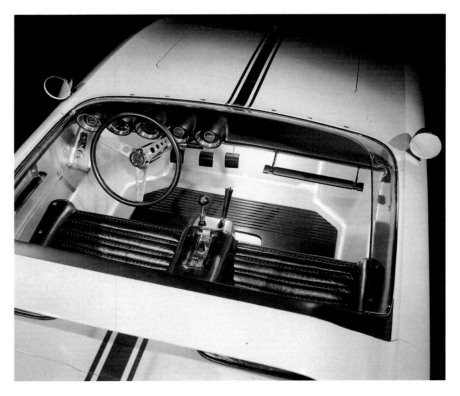

ing all the noise. He is reported to have said in an interview later that the only people saying it was the best car ever built were the automobile enthusiasts. "When I looked at the guys saying it – the offbeat crowd, the real buffs – I said, 'That's sure not the car we want to build, because it can't be a volume car. It's too far out!' "

Certainly in its prototype form, the Mustang I would have been prohibitively expensive to produce because existing technology wasn't geared to mass-produce space-framed cars with aluminum body panels. Even *Autocar* in its summing up admitted that.

So the little Mustang I was a non-starter. Had Ford put it into production, it would almost have certainly stood the world's motoring industry on its head. But Iacocca was adamant it wouldn't work in a mass market, and hindsight tells us that he was probably right. A radical small car such as this wouldn't have suited an America still having an affair with high style. Iacocca's vision saw something more: the dimensions of the original Thunderbird with sharp looks and flair to match.

Funny how tastes change: 25 years later, Pontiac's Fiero sold like hot cakes. Small, mid-engined, all independent suspension and two seats – it's almost as if the Mustang I had made it into production after all.

With the cancellation of the little Mustang I, it was back to the drawing board. Nobody was quite sure what was wanted, or for that matter what exactly was in Iacocca's or the Fairlane committee's collective minds. All that Iacocca was sure about was that he wanted an image builder – but a salable image builder. A sporty car of 1955-57 T-Bird dimensions was mass appeal. There was certainly no shortage of ideas pouring out of Ford's styling studio, and even outsiders were jumping on the bandwagon. One such group was the Budd Body Company.

Budd tooled the bodies for the original T-Bird and still had the dies. A long-established Ford supplier, Budd came up with the XT-Bird and submitted it to Ford for approval. Actually, Budd's proposal was quite workable. What Budd engineers had done was to take a Falcon chassis and marry it to a much modified '57 Thunderbird body. Modifications included shearing off the fins, reshaping the windshield, and lowering the front fenders. A rear jump seat was also added.

Try as they might, Budd executives couldn't convince Ford their XT-Bird was the answer. Although Budd guaranteed completed bodies in six months, its appearance didn't appeal to Ford's hierarchy, so another promising idea went to the scrap heap.

Time was running short by now; it was well into 1962, and Ford management were pinning their hopes on a new car for an introduction in April 1964 which

would coincide with the opening of New York's World's Fair. The Mustang I, still awaiting its PR launch at Watkins Glen, had already been dismissed together with the host of other ideas, with designs and clay models being pumped out by the styling studios.

By now Iacocca and the committee had decided on the sort of car they wanted. It had to be a maximum of 180 inches in overall length; weigh around 2,500 lbs; have a stick shift and four bucket seats – a two-seater car was ruled out as only having limited market appeal. It would also feature exclusive use of Falcon mechanical components to help keep its price down to a projected $2,500, and have styling that said "youthful and sporty." Finally, the car had to have an endless option list that would allow the buyer to build his purchase exactly the way he wanted.

Late summer 1962 and the days were drawing depressingly short. It was at this time that Iacocca decided to hold a competition among Ford's designers. He discussed it with Gene Bordinat, Ford's styling chief, who in turn talked to his top stylists, explaining that their studios would each produce at least one model encompassing all the specifications laid down by Iacocca and the committee. Four Ford styling teams were given the brief and asked to have their clay models ready for review within three weeks.

Working around the clock, the stylists had seven models ready for management assessment within the time allotted. On August 16, 1962, the clays were laid side by side in the Ford Design Center courtyard. Considering the speed with which they sprang from creative minds to drawing boards and finally to clay models, the designs were superb. One, however, was head and shoulders above the rest and was the unanimous choice of those present on that muggy summer's day.

THE CHOSEN MODEL

Designed by Dave Ash, assistant to Ford studio chief Joe Oros, the winning car was based upon the Falcon floorpan. It had a wheelbase of 108 inches, an overall length of 186 inches, some six inches longer than the specifications laid down.

Much of Ash's design was a compilation of various elements taken from other studios' styling efforts. Easy to spot were the Mustang I's side scoops. The Cougar, as it was initially called, was also designed to accept either Ford's V8 or standard six. The Cougar's design, which much impressed Iacocca, was very similar to the eventual 1964½ Mustang. Only the frontal area and tail section were modified on the production car; most of the design went through intact. For one reason or another, the Cougar's name was altered to Torino, then shortly after to

LEFT ABOVE. The drawing of the galloping Mustang pony toward the right was done by John Najjar. When the pony appeared on the car, it was galloping to the left. Najjar said later that he is left-handed and it was easier for him to draw lines flowing from the right, hence the original drawing. Gene Bordinat was right-handed so perhaps he viewed the emblem the way he would have drawn it. Perhaps the decision was made because western languages are read from left to right, or because heraldic animals usually face left.

ABOVE. Developed by stylist Don DeLaRossa from sketches made by John Najjar, the Mustang II was conceived by Gene Bordinat after the production Mustang had been approved. The Mustang II was created to prepare the consumer for the forthcoming production car.

LEFT BELOW. A 1963 Ford Falcon. Much of the original production Mustang was based on Ford's popular compact.

Mustang II. At this time the name Mustang had not yet been chosen for the car that would make its way into production.

Encouraged by their proposal's success, Oros' team designed an exciting two-seater not unlike the Corvette Stingray and called it the Cougar II. A running prototype was constructed, but it fared no better than the Mustang I. Management gave it the thumbs down because they still believed a two-seater wouldn't sell in great enough volume to make production worthwhile. Like the Mustang I, the Cougar II was an advanced concept, although the engine – a 260-cubic-inch V8 – was conventionally laid out and drove the rear wheels.

As for the Mustang II, Lee Iacocca had to convince Ford's senior executives and accountants that this car was what the company was waiting for – and needed! Ford, however, had already committed itself to a major retooling of the 1965 models and this fact could have proved a serious obstacle to producing the Mustang. Even Iacocca's persuasive, down-to-earth rhetoric wouldn't be enough on its own to sway the staid traditionalists at the top of the hierarchy. The men at the top listened, howev-

er, and were quite optimistic, and a full study of Iacocca's proposal was ordered. Fortunately for Lee, he had one strong ally, the most important ally of all. That was Henry Ford II himself. He liked the idea and liked the car. Even though the results of the study projected sales of 86,000, which might conceivably take away sales from established lines, Project T-5 was approved on September 10, 1962, for production engineering.

ARRIVAL AT WATKINS GLEN

A running prototype of the Oros car was wheeled out to be shown at Watkins Glen before the 1963 Grand Prix. By the time the Mustang II prototype was shown, the production Mustang was well on its way to finalization and the assembly lines. The prototype itself attracted much attention on the day, and one wonders how many who saw it guessed they were having a sneak preview of the shape of things to come, albeit in slightly modified form.

One and a half years doesn't sound too long to design and engineer an automobile from prototype to production car, but in the Mustang's case everything was accomplished without too much difficulty. The reasons for this are not hard to find. For one thing, the Oros design survived development almost intact, and it was only a case of engineering the body to take existing Falcon/Fairlane components such as engines, drivetrain, suspensions and chassis. Making use of existing, off-the-shelf components had the advantage of proven reliability as well as negating the huge costs involved in engineering from scratch. Purists might have been dubious, but building the Mustang this way kept its overall cost per unit within the parameters of its final retail price of $2,500.

Everything was going to plan with the exception of one important point: the name. No one had come up with anything suitable. Several titles had been bandied

ABOVE AND RIGHT. Two more views of the first Mustang which, as can be seen, was a convertible. It was bought by airline pilot Captain Stan Tucker. (Photos courtesy The Henry Ford Museum & Greenfield Village.)

around; some of them used before on the different design exercises created for the T-5 project. Names like Allegro, Cougar, Torino, even Mustang. Henry Ford suggested it be called the Thunderbird II, or even just T-Bird II, but nobody liked that one, even if the Boss did. Fortunately, Henry Ford didn't lose any sleep over it so the hunt for the name continued.

At this point Iacocca called in John Conley, from J. Walter Thompson, Ford's ad agency. Conley was a dab hand at dreaming up names – he had found the Falcon name which was used on Ford's 1960 compact. So he started researching at the Detroit Public Library, looking for animal names, which were Iacocca's preference. After plowing through animal names from A to Z, Conley narrowed the field down to six: Bronco, Puma, Cheetah, Colt, Mustang and Cougar. It is also said he added Pinto and Maverick, both names, along with Bronco, that would turn up on future Ford products.

There must have been a feeling of deja vu when the name Mustang came out as the winner. After all it had been used on two prototypes. It had romantic appeal, the ad-men said, it conjured up images of wide open spaces, of cowboys and wild horses galloping fast and free. Everybody liked the sound of that, and it is surprising nobody thought of Mustang in those terms before. Strange as it may seem, when the title had been applied to the two Mustang prototypes, it had been used because it reminded the stylists of the legendary American World War II fighter plane. John Najjar, who thought of the Mustang name first, admits he associated it with the P.51 Mustang, an aircraft he greatly admired. When the name had been considered in that light, management drew back because the last thing they wanted was a warlike image. But horses, sunsets, prairies, that's different. That was the stuff of American romance.

On March 9, 1964, the first production Mustang rolled off the assembly line. 571 days had passed since the Oros design had been selected. The car was everything Iacocca had envisaged it to be. It had style, the right price, and youthful appeal written all over it. Prior to its launch, a market survey had been conducted in Ford's styling studio. Fifty-two couples, of mixed income, all car owners, had been invited to view a Mustang prototype. The higher income couples were impressed with its design. So were the lower income couples, who saw it as a symbol of status. Asked what price it was, everybody was above target. When told its actual cost, any inhibitions they may have had over price disappeared. They all wanted the car.

Launch date was fast approaching. Iacocca fervently hoped the 52 couples' reaction would be endemic to the rest of America. He would know soon enough.

LEFT. *Mustangs roll off the production line in readiness for their April 17, 1964, launch.*

RIGHT. *The very first Mustang to be built, Production Mustang No. 1, resides today at the Henry Ford Museum in Dearborn, Michigan.*

2
EVERYBODY WANTS TO RIDE THE PONY

Everybody knew about April 17. Everybody knew that Ford dealerships, airport terminals, Holiday Inn lobbies would be displaying the new Mustang. And if they didn't, they should have been ashamed of themselves! For the Mustang launch was one of the biggest media events in motoring history; one of the worst-kept new car secrets ever – accidentally on purpose, of course!

The rumor mills in the automotive press had been fed tantalizing leaks for months beforehand; press baiting had become the norm at Ford. *Time* magazine was in on the "secret" from the early design days of the Mustang II prototype; a *Time* photographer was on call to record its development to the finished product. The editors promised not to release anything in return for the story and they stood by their word. *Time* had hoped for a scoop, but the week it ran the feature as a cover story, *Time's* greatest rival *Newsweek* ran a cover story on Lee Iacocca and the Mustang. In the week before the Mustang went on sale, every major U.S. journal and newspaper carried feature articles on the car. So big was the story that it made copy in several overseas publications as well.

An estimated 30 million people saw the Mustang unveiled on the evening of April 16. Ford had bought the 9 P.M. prime time–slot on all three major TV networks, and the next day 2,600 newspapers carried advertisements and articles that spread the car's image coast to coast. Ford gave selected college newspaper editors a Mustang each to drive for a few weeks, and 100 motor-

ing journalists lived it up at Ford's expense before each was given a chance to drive a Mustang 700 miles, from the World's Fair headquarters in New York to Dearborn. It was a clever PR gimmick to demonstrate the Mustang's reliability, an exercise that could have gone embarrassingly wrong. It didn't, much to the relief of everyone concerned; each Mustang completed the course without the slightest hint of trouble. Even if the purists were a little disappointed that the Mustang was conventional rather than advanced like the Mustang I prototype, which had lifted hopes so high, they had to admit that for the money it was a fine and promising new car.

Before launch day, 8,160 Mustangs were built to guarantee that every Ford dealer in the United States had at least one in his showroom. When April 17 finally dawned, even the most hardened salesmen were bowled over by the stampede into their showrooms. They couldn't remember a time when one car generated so much excitement. Over four million people visited Ford dealerships during the first weekend the Mustang was on sale and you may have heard the story of the dealer in Garland, Texas, who had 15 people bidding for his solitary Mustang. He sold it to the highest bidder who stayed all night in the car while his check was clearing, to make sure nobody else would buy it! He's become a legend now. Then there's the Chicago dealer who became so apprehensive of the huge crowd outside that he locked his showroom doors! Those are the famous stories; certainly there were others we haven't heard about.

LEFT. All the world loves a Mustang. The Mustang Club of America boasts members from Australia to Sweden. This nice Springtime Yellow 1965 fastback resides in England.

ABOVE. One of the earliest Mustangs. Built on April 4, 1964, this hardtop features the 260 cubic inch, 164 bhp V8. The engine was dropped in September 1964 in favor of a 2v 289 rated at 200 bhp. Cars with the 260 V8 are quite rare today.

TOP. *Waiting for the train that might never come, a Guardsman Blue 1965 Mustang convertible basks in the late afternoon sun.*

ABOVE. *A standard wheel cover fitted 13- or 14-inch wheels, but there were five optional covers to choose*

from. Simulated air intakes adorn each side of the grille which is flanked by single headlights (right). Tri-taillight assembly (above) is attractive but is actually one unit and is recessed into the rear panel. The deck-mounted luggage rack (above right) was an option.

ABOVE. Dished color-keyed steering wheel was standard in this form. A woodgrain walnut-effect wheel could be had if the buyer specified the Interior Decor Group.

ABOVE LEFT. An attractive interior was considered marred by the Falcon-style dashboard and some criticized the simulated rear scoop (left).

FAITH REPAID

Dealers couldn't get Mustangs fast enough; all the launch cars sold in a matter of days, even hours. Nobody cared about the car's base price, a mere $2,368, and most of the early Mustangs sold way above retail. Lee Iacocca's hunch had paid off handsomely. "The market which had been looking for a car, has it now," enthused *Car Life* magazine. Back in Dearborn, Iacocca's name took on messianic proportions: he was the hero of the hour. None of the team involved in creating the Mustang, not even Iacocca, who had more faith in the car than anyone, could estimate that 100,000 Mustangs would sell within the first four months. To cater for the extraordinary demand, Iacocca switched the Ford assembly plant in San Jose, California, over to Mustang production.

The enormous media coverage organized by Ford must have cost almost as much as developing the Mustang itself. It was a brilliant campaign, which certainly more than played its part in drumming up such widespread interest. Iacocca himself credits *Time* and *Newsweek* for selling an additional 100,000 cars with their excellent coverage of the project. *Time* likened the Mustang to a Ferrari for the masses, and one gets the feeling both magazines were as pleased as Ford that the car was a phenomenal success.

Considering the lack of models at the time of launch – only two were offered, a hardtop and convertible – its instant success shows just how impressive the Mustang was. From a first-year target of below 100,000, Iacocca now had his sights on overhauling the Falcon's first-year sales of a record 417,174 cars. He needn't have worried: on April 16, 1965, a young Californian walked into his local showroom and bought Mustang number 418,812. That was almost half a million cars in 12 months, setting a record which wasn't broken until the early Seventies by Ford's compact Maverick.

It doesn't take much to understand why the Mustang did so well and sold in such numbers. It was – and still is – a handsome, well-proportioned automobile designed without a lot of unnecessary adornment. It was the right size at the right price, and it scored a bulls-eye in the marketplace. The razzmatazz that preceded and surrounded it, as well as its stylish, youthful demeanor, all echoed the Detroit of the mid-Fifties and proved that Iacocca had his roots in that period. Not since that decade had there been such joyous enthusiasm generated around a new car. Overnight the Mustang had become a legend as strong and as desirable as the Ferrari. And at a base price of $2,368, who could argue?

What of the car itself? Was it really worth all the fuss?

By and large, the author thinks it certainly was. As noted above, the Mustang was a very attractive-looking machine. Its long hood and short deck design made it stand out from the crowd. The front had a simple, open-mouthed grille, a blue/gray-painted honeycomb behind a horizontal chrome bar, the middle of which is the Mustang's emblem, a galloping pony set inside a corral matching the grille's outline. You will notice the pony is galloping from right to left: apparently it wasn't meant to be. According to some sources, the pony was originally meant to run left to right. It was only when production was underway that the stylists realized the mistake. At this point there was nothing anyone could do about it, so it was left to run the wrong way forever.

The other explanation comes from Lee Iacocca's book, where he says that, although folks like to point out the traditional way for horses to gallop is counterclockwise, as at race tracks, his answer has always been the Mustang is a wild horse, not a tamed racer; therefore it would run whichever way it chose. "I felt increasingly sure that it was headed in the right direction," he concluded – a perfectly logical answer from a man who always had the Mustang's direction close to his heart.

ABOVE. The most popular engine in the Mustang line-up was the 289. It came in 2 or 4v guise, and a 271 bhp high-performance version was offered later in 1964.

LEFT. Mustang versus Mustang, both legends in their time. A World War II P.51 Mustang fighter stands alongside a 1965 Mustang 2+2 fastback. The warlike image attached to the P.51 was considered as the icon for the car, but it lost out to the pony, which conveyed the feeling Ford wanted to attach to its creation.

*A pristine example of a 1965
Mustang convertible powered by a
289 V8. This one is loaded with the
options current in 1965.*

MUSTANG STYLE

A holdover from the Mustang I was the sculptured styling on the sides of the car, starting at the front fender's leading edge, becoming more pronounced as it progressed, and ending in a scoop ahead of the rear wheel openings. A fake air intake in chrome accentuates the scoop, which was left off the fastback bodystyle when it was added to the line in September 1964. Behind the front wheel opening is the word "Mustang" preceded by a red, white and blue vertical bar with the galloping pony cast on top.

Bumpers with admittedly dubious protection properties were fitted almost flush, front and rear, with two chrome vertical bars beneath the front bumper, breaking up the valance which highlights the front's sporty appearance. The word "Ford" is written in block capitals across the front leading edge of the hood, while the only identification adorning the attractive and sporty kicked-up rear is what looks like a bright metal, die-cast medallion with the pony and bar embossed on a black ceramic center. The words "Ford" and "Mustang" are stamped on the medal-

lion's circular perimeter in black and red respectively. Actually this device is the gas filler cap and is centered between what appear to be three vertical taillight covers positioned just inboard of the rear fender caps. In fact, it is a clever optical illusion; each taillight assembly is made of a single lens covered by a chromed frame with two raised centrally located vertical strips, the whole unit held in place by four screws.

The 1964½ (actually 1965 models according to Ford) Mustang hardtop roof featured a delicately sculptured concave indentation starting at the base of the rear pillars and following the rear window outline. It was little touches like this that gave the Mustang an air of expensive elegance belying its price. Unfortunately, the air of elegance literally took a nose-dive at the front of the car, which was marred by generally poor-fitting fender caps (housing the single headlights) and grille frame. Of the hood fit, *Car and Driver* said it reminded them "of the lid on one of our mother's more experienced saucepans," in reference to the way in which the hood closed. In fairness, the car was new, and many of these shortcomings were

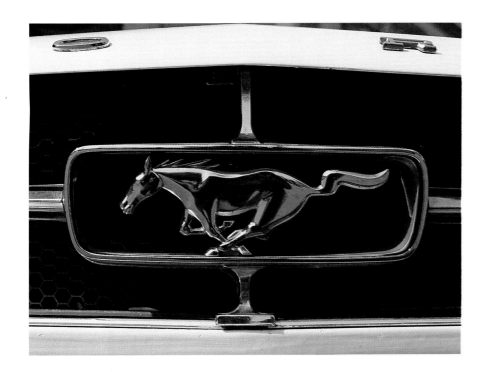

ABOVE. The pony that was to run the wrong way forever more. As Lee Iacocca said, a pony gallops every which way.

LEFT. Any street anywhere in the U.S.A. would have had a Mustang parked somewhere in 1965. Here's a splendid '65 hardtop re-living those bygone days.

ABOVE. *Whatever the setting, a Mustang never looks out of place. Imagine owning a car as beautiful as this! This '65 fastback is today worth more to collectors than the hardtop. Only 77,000 were built compared to almost 465,000 hardtops in '64/'65; hence its desirability.*

RIGHT. *The interior shows off the walnut woodgrain rimmed steering wheel, which tells us this Mustang has the Interior Decor package.*

LEFT. Like a butterfly emerging into the light of a summer's day, a 1965 fastback gets ready to roll. The non-standard wheels are an example of the many accessories that followed Mustang onto the market.

improved once production got into its stride, eventually disappearing altogether when the restyled Mustangs of 1967 arrived.

The interior of the 1965 Mustang combined sporty flavor and small family-car comfort. Nicely styled, thin-shell bucket seats were standard for driver and front passenger – a front bench was optional though few took it up – while a bench-type seat designed to look like buckets filled the rear. Five choices of all-vinyl upholstery were offered, as well as two cloth and vinyl combinations at no extra cost. The colors offered, were black, white, blue, red and palomino. Front–seat room was comfortable, but back-seat passengers might have found it a tight squeeze on long journeys.

Ahead of the driver, the instrument cluster was universally regarded as a bit of a disappointment in a car supposedly sporty in character. For the horizontal bezel with a speedometer (the pods contained fuel gauge on the left, temperature on the right) appears to have been lifted almost intact from the Falcon, though different set-ups could be ordered from the long options list. On the other hand, the steering wheel, a Mustang original as far as one could tell, was deeply dished with three center spokes, the latter covered by a matching chrome horn ring with simulated hole, no doubt to remind the owner that he was driving a sports car! Or a car with sporty looks. Finally, the steering wheel hub was embossed with much the same motif as the gas filler cap; a pony atop a

red, white and blue vertical strip with the words "Ford" and "Mustang" stamped on the perimeter.

Full wall-to-wall color-keyed carpeting, floor shift lever, seat belts, and thick crash padding on top of the instrument panel were all standard fare, but the extensive options list meant the owner could turn his Mustang into a full-blooded sports car – on the inside at least – and as we shall see, the options didn't stop there.

The Mustang employed a platform frame with strong side rails complete with five welded crossmembers for additional strength. Body panels were welded to the platform forming an integral steel structure. A full-depth cowl formed a box section housing the engine, to which were bolted the front fenders. A heavier-gauge steel was used on the platform structure if the model was a convertible.

As mentioned earlier, most of the Mustang's mechanical components were shared with the Falcon and Fairlane, though it was the Falcon's parts bin that was most heavily cannibalized. Front suspension, which consisted of an upper wishbone and lower central arm, an anti-roll bar, coil springs and telescopic shocks, were lifted directly from the Falcon. Different forward spring mountings, stronger rubber bump stops, and slightly stiffer leaf springs were all that distinguished the rear suspension from the standard Falcon settings. However, an optional handling package was offered for improved handling, but was standardized for use with the high performance 289 V8 (of which more later).

Initially Mustangs were equipped with one of three engines. Standard was the Falcon-derived 170 cubic-inch, 101 bhp straight six coupled to Falcon's three speed manual transmission, but with the floor-mounted shift. Fairlane provided the 260 cubic-inch, 160 bhp V8. Called the Challenger, the 260 had the three speed manual transmission as standard, but Ford's Cruise-O-Matic three-speed automatic was there if anyone wanted it – and a lot did! Cruise-O-Matic was an option on all engines including the 289 cubic-inch, 200 bhp V8 with a two-barrel carburetor. A four-barrel version of the 289 was also available with an increased horsepower of 210 bhp as well as a 9:1 compression ratio. Both 289s had a four-speed, all-synchro manual transmission, as well as a transmission with three speeds, all synchro, and the Cruise-O-Matic. For some curious reason never fully explained, the six cylinder's three-speed transmission was non-synchromesh in first gear, which meant drivers who did a lot of gear changing needed to learn how to double-declutch from their grandfathers!

Early Mustang catalogs spoke of a high-performance

289 V8 being prepared for in June 1964. As promised, it arrived on time and proved a very potent package. It developed 271 bhp at 6,000 rpm, and 312 ft/lbs of torque at 3,400 rpm. The engine featured a high-compression cylinder head, high-lift camshaft, chrome-plated valve stems and solid valve lifters among other fittings. Compression ratio was 10.5:1 and the engine came with a single four-barrel carburetor. Although advertised as a 271 bhp unit, it has been pointed out that Ford tested the engine, complete with ancillaries on a dynomometer and only managed to get 232 bhp at 5,500 rpm. This is the true reading, but the advertised figure was obtained from a block minus ancillary equipment. Nowadays, the manufacturers advertise the net horsepower from the complete engine as the customer would buy it, but in the past it was the gross horsepower from a stripped engine that was quoted – as in the case of the Mustang.

Not that it mattered one iota. The fact remains that the high-performance 289 engine was lethal indeed. It had been designed in 1958/59 by George F. Stirrat. A

RIGHT. A 1965 Mustang fastback receiving admiring attention from a group of its namesakes. To capture the spirit of eternal youth, to run wild, to run free with the herd; that's what Mustang is all about.

BELOW RIGHT. Another example of the 1965 Mustang fastback, painted honey gold. This one is a six-cylinder version, as can be seen by the lack of any ornamentation forward of the front fender wheelwell.

major advantage was its lightweight cast-iron construction (it weighed in complete at only 450 pounds) and compact (8.93 inches high, 16.36 inches wide and 20.48 inches long) dimensions. It first appeared in 221 cubic-inch form in 1961 and grew from there.

Only one transmission came with the high-performance 289 in its first year. This was a close-ration four-speed manual which was exclusive to the high-performance 289. Standard rear-axle ratio was 3.50, although 3.89 and 4.11 were options for the drag racing circuit.

Standard on Mustangs ordered with this engine was the handling suspension. It consisted of up-rated springs and shocks and had a larger front anti-roll bar. Even if the handling package wasn't standard with this particular engine, it only cost $31 and was worth every cent. Other desirable – and necessary – extras were the Rally-Pac, consisting of rev-counter and clock, quicker steering, and 5.90x15 Firestone Super Sports tires, (far safer than the standard 6.50x13s they would replace).

ABOVE AND CENTRE. Right from the start, Mustangs were entered into competition. Here's a 1966 fastback in racing hue. Note the absence of front and rear bumpers, which were more for show than for protection.

TOP. The front fenders of early Mustangs equipped with a V8 came with a "V"-shaped ornament denoting engine size.

THESE PAGES. *To celebrate sales of one million Mustangs, Ford offered a specially equipped, limited-edition model. Special equipment included the Sprint 200 Option Group consisting of wire wheel covers, accent stripe, chrome air cleaner and center console. Also featured was the Safety Equipment Group including padded instrument panel, seatbelts front and rear, back-up lights and emergency flasher. The standard engine was the 200 cid 120 bhp six. Note that the Sprint 200 Group did away with the simulated rear scoop.*

INSET ABOVE. *Although mechanically identical to any other six-cylinder equipped Mustang, the Limited Edition model was set apart by chrome air cleaner and unique decal which read MUSTANG POWERED SPRINT 200.*

INSET FAR RIGHT. *The deluxe optional steering wheel featured simulated walnut applique studded with 18 bright recessed dots and brushed metal spokes with 12 circular holes. Wow!*

THE PRESS RESPONDS

The September 1964 issue of *Sports Car Graphic* had a high-performance Mustang on test. It was loaded with all performance options including the 271 bhp 289 and the items listed above. It also had a radio and wire wheels. Remember that the base 100 bhp six-cylinder Mustang retailed at $2,368. *Sports Car Graphic* editors found their test car with all the above options came to $3,854! The magazine thought this a "not unreasonable figure compared with the 'performance' cars built in Michigan." The author would go further and say it was a bargain when compared to performance cars from Europe!

Those early Mustangs had one drawback that could have proved hazardous in the wrong hands, especially V8-powered models. The cars had no brakes to speak of. Well, they had drums with a 10-inch diameter, which were probably all right with the six-cylinder models, but worse than useless trying to stop power-plus Mustangs. Road tests found the front drums faded to nothing after only two or three panic stops. To their eternal credit, Ford engineers rectified this problem within months of the car's introduction; for $58 extra a customer could specify front disks. These were Kelsey-Hayes disks with a 10-inch diameter, and they made all the difference to the car's

stopping power. At first these brakes weren't power-assisted, but this feature was introduced later.

It is interesting to note what the automotive press really thought of the Mustang. Overall, they liked it, albeit with reservations. *Motor Trend* was disappointed the car didn't evolve from the radical Mustang I. "A nice looking Falcon," they called it, but admitted the Mustang would "sell like proverbial hot cakes." How right they were! *Car & Driver* was kinder in its report. The magazine thought it "Easily the best thing to come out of Dearborn since the 1932 V8 Model B roadster." And they liked its size and "sensible proportions." Even that venerable institution *Road & Track* gave it faint praise, arguing that it was "definitely a sportscar" in the MG-B, Triumph Spitfire tradition, and considered Ford's time well spent in creating the car. The Australian magazine *Modern Motor* unreservedly welcomed the Mustang, praising its looks, feel on the road, and the concept as "an inexpensive status symbol car." As for the ever-reserved British, they weren't quite sure what to make of it, but popped out of their shells long enough to give it good marks even if they didn't care for the car's low gearing, drum brakes, and its attitude in the wet; though both *Autocar and Motor*, who road-tested their respective Mustangs in the fall, reckoned that the disk brakes then available would make all the difference. Still, both magazines were quite impressed with the car which, *Autocar* claimed, only cost around $5 million from creation to production.

In September 1964 a 2 + 2 fastback body style was added to the line-up, which now consisted of three models. The simulated rear fender air scoop was conspicuous by its absence, and buyers of the hardtop coupe and convertible could rid themselves of it if they ordered the "Accent Group" trim option. This replaced the scoop with what was called a "Tiffany" stripe, which followed the body sculpturing contours. Is it possible the designers weren't too sure about its desirability?

After September, shortly after the fastback's debut, the 260 cid small-block Challenger V8 was dropped from the Mustang's engine line-up. Thereafter, the reliable and strong 200 bhp 289 became the basic optional V8, which is hardly surprising because more Mustangs were sold with this engine than any other. With a 0-60 time of about 12 seconds and fuel consumption averaging around 17 miles to the gallon – some claim it will do 20 plus if driven sensibly – allied to a top speed of something approaching 110 mph, this was a little jewel of an engine capable of running 100,000 miles and more with little or no trouble. No other car-making country in the world has been able to build V8 engines as well as the United States, and the 289 is an excellent example of the breed.

Another casualty was the 170 cubic-inch six. This was put out to grass at the same time as the 260 in favor of a longer, 200 cid in-line six. Using a single one-barrel carburetor, the new engine developed 120 bhp and could do the 0-60 in 13-15 seconds. This engine was more robust than its predecessor and had seven main bearings compared to the earlier unit's four.

ABOVE. Functional air extractor vents were a part of the fastback package. In GT form with the optional 271 bhp, 289 Hi-Po V8 and special handling package, the 1966 fastback was, and still is, a most desirable machine.

RIGHT. The long hood, short deck theme is readily apparent in this view of a 1966 Mustang hardtop coupe.

Now–just in time for Christmas–
only at your Ford Dealer's!

MIDGET MUSTANG

Specially priced at only

$12.95

While they last!

Here's a child's gift that'll look just as inviting under a Christmas tree as a 1965 Mustang will look in your driveway. The solid, all-metal Midget Mustang, that you might expect to see offered for $25.00, has easy-to-use pedals, make-believe shift lever and real rubber tires. Give your child a Midget Mustang this Christmas—for a taste of the fun all Mustangers enjoy! Stop in at your participating Ford Dealer's and pick one up for only $12.95, suggested list price . . . , at no obligation. For $2.00 more, dealer can order for delivery to your doorstep.

Best year yet to go Ford

MUSTANG!
MUSTANG!
MUSTANG!

Gift idea for the whole family! 1965 Mustang—the most successful new car ever introduced in America!

Two weeks ago this man was a bashful schoolteacher in a small mid-western city. Add Mustang.
Now he has three steady girls, is on first name terms with the best headwaiter in town, is society's darling. All the above came with his Mustang. So did bucket seats, full wheel covers, wall-to-wall carpeting, padded dash, vinyl upholstery, and more. Join the Mustangers!
Enjoy a lot of *dolce vita* at a low, low price.

Best year yet to go Ford!
Test Drive Total Performance '65

FORD

ABOVE LEFT. Mustang mania even extended to kids. Of course, they couldn't drive dad's Mustang, so Ford offered a pedal-propelled model just in time for Christmas 1965. A way, perhaps, to guarantee a future Mustang buyer? Who said catch 'em while they're young?

ABOVE RIGHT. One of a series of advertisements extolling Mustang's virtues. Not that anybody needed telling ... one look at the car alone was enough to convince most potential buyers!

RIGHT. In 1966, 64,990 Mustang convertibles like this one were produced. Whichever way you look at this car, it looks right. It says a lot for the car's timeless design.

THE BUYERS DECIDE

After the car had been on the market for a while, some interesting facts regarding buyer preferences began to emerge. Ford research discovered 71 percent ordered V8 engines, 80 percent took radios, and another 80 percent specified whitewall tires. Fifty percent ordered automatic transmissions; this was quite a low figure, which went to prove a large proportion of the buyers were young and more likely to opt for sportier manual transmissions. One in ten was ordered with the Rally-Pac.

One reason for the Mustang's outstanding success was its huge list of options, allowing the buyer to tailor his car any way he wanted. Then there was an almost infinite number of dealer-installed accessories, and it wasn't long before after-market accessories began to appear in auto stores and on K-Mart shelves. Bearing in mind the wealth of add-ons, put-ins and go-fasters on offer, it is highly likely there are no two Mustangs exactly alike. With a $2,368 base price, Ford found buyers were spending an extra $1,000 on options alone.

Because of its early introduction – at least five months ahead of the traditional fall new-car announcements – the 1965 Mustang's run was longer than a normal car's season. From April 1964 to August 1965, the 1964½ and 1965 Mustang had a staggering "model year production" figure of 680,989. Categorized into models, the Mustang sold in the following numbers: (The number before each model type indicates Mustang body-style codes.)

63A Fastback, standard 71,303
63B Fastback, deluxe 5,776
65A Hardtop, standard 464,828
65B Hardtop, deluxe 22,232
65C Hardtop, bench seats 14,905
76A Convertible, standard 94,496
76B Convertible, deluxe 5,338
76C Convertible, bench seats 2,111
TOTAL 680,989

The most popular was the hardtop, least desirable the bench-seated convertible. Possibly the rarest 1964½ Mustang is the 260 V8 version. It is distinguished by a front fender "V"-shaped motif with the numbers "260" denoting engine size, above the "V". This is also used to identify the 289, while the 271 bhp 289 has the words "High Performance" etched in black on satin and flanked by checkered symbols above the 289 number.

The Mustang was the populist flagship of Ford's Total Performance program and succeeded in turning Ford's dowdy old-maid image into that of an aggressive, young-at-heart go-getter. Nothing helped more than the Indianapolis 500, where Mustang was selected as the 1964 Pace Car. Lee Iacocca was reputed to have described the Mustang as a historic landmark sharing its place with the Model A and Model T. Nobody can argue with that; the Mustang revolutionized American driving, and nothing has been quite the same ever since.

*ABOVE. **The clean, uncluttered lines of the 1966 Mustang won millions of admirers – and the same holds true today.***

3
SNAKES ALIVE – SHELBY STYLE!

otal Performance, that was Ford's name for a new game it was playing. Under Iacocca, the company's premier division threw away its staid, McNamara-inspired image, turning its back on the AMA racing ban to which all American manufacturers had given voluntary – if not entirely strict – support since 1958 and went racing in a big way. There's nothing new about car manufacturers going into competition. It's been done ever since the first cars took to the road, because first and foremost a car maker who wins competitions sells more of his products. Not only that, but racing, hill climbing, stock car racing, and anything else competitive points to improvements and gives customers safer, more reliable automobiles.

So Ford hit the circuits, the hill climbs and rallies, spending millions of dollars to guarantee success that would translate into more units off the showroom floor. Europe was a major target in classic events like the Monte Carlo Rally, Le Mans and the Tour de France, which were dominated by European breeds. Ford in its

first year walked away with an outstanding class win when a team of Falcons sailed through the Monte Carlo Rally. Mustangs also took the touring category in the Tour de France. Two years later, Le Mans would fall. A one-two-three win with Holman-Moody and Shelby-built Ford GT40s raised the Stars and Stripes over hallowed ground, trouncing Ferraris and Porsches in their wake.

Carroll Hall Shelby is one of the names associated with Ford's historic Le Mans winning team. Mere mention of Carroll Shelby in company of sports-car and racing enthusiasts around the world elicits a response not unlike spontaneous combustion.

Americans eulogize about him, this tall, wavy-haired Texan who had the effrontery to challenge Europe's four-wheeled gods of the track – and win. As with most things concerning driving, nobody begrudges a winner, especially a winner like Shelby. Even Europe, home of great motor-racing legends, has a high regard for Carroll Hall Shelby and his achievements both on and off the competition circuits.

LEFT. A man and his machines. One-time chicken farmer, racing driver and ultimately car builder, the legendary Carroll Shelby is father of the equally legendary AC Cobra and the fabulous Shelby-Mustang. Here is the great man standing near Los Angeles Airport with a 1968 Shelby GT-350 and GT-500.

ABOVE. Original ACs continued to be built at Shelby's California plant alongside Shelby-Mustangs, albeit in very limited quantities. With body designed and produced by AC Cars in England and running gear by Shelby, the Cobra has become one of the great classics of the postwar period. This particular model, a 1966 Cobra, is powered by Ford's 289 V8, the same engine used in Mustang.

ABOVE. *Another view of the Cobra 289, a true classic in every way.*

MAKING THE GRADE

With none of the advantages of an inherited bankroll and no personal fortune to dip into, Carroll Shelby made it the hard way. Born and raised in East Texas, he worked at everything from truck driver to chicken farmer. Possessed of an innate talent for driving, Shelby first took a shot at competition racing in the early Fifties. He drove MGs at first, and it wasn't long before he had graduated to the "hard stuff" and was making a name for himself at the wheel of Ferraris.

Before long, Shelby came to the attention of the British Aston-Martin Car Company, who signed him up in 1954 as a driver for the works team. He was 31 and had come a long way from his first competition event in a friend's MG, in Norman, Oklahoma, just two years previously.

By 1957 Shelby was internationally recognized as a world-class driver. To prove the point, he won the SCCA crown for the second year in a row, taking first place 19 times in the championship. It wasn't all a bed of roses, though: in September 1957 he sustained severe injuries in a crash at Riverside Raceway, resulting in facial plastic surgery and other corrective work. However, he was back in the driver's seat the following season, good as new, and in 1959 was one of the drivers who guided Aston-Martin home to win the classic 24-hour Le Mans endurance race.

Trouble was brewing, however. Shelby had a feeling all was not well within himself. Consulting his doctor, he was given the shattering news that his heart wasn't all that it should have been. He was advised to quit while he was still ahead. For an all-action man like Shelby, this must have been hard to do, but true to his Texas stock, he wasn't stopping now. Racing, yes, but racing cars and particularly sports cars, most certainly not. He had plans, big plans.

Like many others before him, Shelby decided that southern California's balmy climate of sun and sea was the place to live. He bought a Goodyear tire distributorship and set up shop in Gardena, a few miles from Santa Fe Springs. This was quite fortuitous in the Shelby saga, because Santa Fe Springs happened to be the location of a Firestone tire dealership run by an old friend of his, Dean Moon. In fact, Shelby had first moved his tire business into the same premises which Moon occupied, until Goodyear, quite understandably, took a dim view of cohabiting with a major rival and told Shelby to relocate elsewhere.

LEFT. The fiberglass front spoiler was not a standard accessory, but it adds to the car's overall effect.

LEFT. Body style differed little from the Mustang fastback in 1965, but Plexiglass rear quarter windows were unique to '66 Shelbys.

LEFT. White with blue striping was the only color available for 1965 Shelby GT-350. In 1966 several color choices were offered: stripes on all other colors were white and blue stripes on white cars.

ENTER AC

In 1962 Derek Hurlock's little car business was in deep trouble. His company, AC Cars Ltd., of Thames Ditton, Surrey, England, had been making lightweight sports cars for about 35 years, built in limited numbers and aimed at the wealthier end of the market. Until 1962, AC had relied on engines provided by another specialist car firm with a strong pedigree. This was Bristol, maker of the fabulous 401 coupe and a subsidiary of the Bristol Aeroplane Company. Both AC and Bristol had made their own engines at one time, which was fine when production hovered around the three-figure mark, but decidedly uneconomical when they were building only four or five dozen cars in any one year. AC stopped building engines first, hence the reliance on Bristol. When Bristol, too, found limited engine production uneconomical, the plug was pulled. Bristol went elsewhere, finally deciding on Chrysler V8s, but AC was left high and dry with a lot of spare chassis and bodies, but no engines to put in them. Hurlock was just about to call it a day when salvation came along with a deep Texan drawl.

AC's plight coincided with Ford's development of its lightweight 260 cid V8 engine. It had started out life as a 221 cubic-inch unit for the Fairlane model line-up. As engines go, it was soon recognized as one of the best powerplants around, and Ford was quick to realize its potential. So did Carroll Shelby, who saw the chance to build himself a meaty sports car by combining Ford's engine with AC's chassis and body. Using all the natural charm he could muster plus the merest hint of a white lie, Shelby contacted Ford and told them he had chassis and bodies just begging for Ford's 260. He didn't have any at the time, but he then telephoned AC and told them the same tale – in reverse.

His tongue-in-cheek gamble paid off and his timing couldn't have been better. Ford, now deeply enmeshed in its Total Performance program, wanted a test bed and the competition publicity Shelby's venture could supply. AC, on the other hand, simply wanted to survive for another day. The Shelby name was known and trusted; both parties saw the plan as advantageous, albeit for different reasons, and to Shelby's obvious delight as well as relief, they both agreed to his requests.

Next step was to obtain financial credit for the operation, which began its life on Dean Moon's premises. Now all that was left was to build the car. Shelby had the engines; he had the bodies. Soón the first Cobra, with Shelby and Moon as driver and passenger, roared off into the night, twisting and turning, accelerating and wheeling until the excitement leveled off and a new dawn was perhaps breaking the sky. Significant, perhaps, for the new dawn was to be Carroll Shelby's, too.

ABOVE. 1965-67 Shelby GT Mustangs are worth their weight in gold these days and for good reason. Note the Shelby rocker covers. The VIN plate says it all: it means any car with this ID is a genuine California-built Shelby car.

RIGHT. A 289 Mustang V8 after the Selby treatment. In Shelby guise, this engine was a stormer on both road and track.

The wheel center cap clearly shows what car this is. A 9,000 tachometer sits atop the dashboard and competition seatbelts show this is not a car for the faint of heart.

*ABOVE AND RIGHT. **1966 Shelby GT350 in traditional blue and white American racing colors.***

DREAMING COBRA

As legend has it, Shelby's choice of name for his hybrid car came to him in a dream. He awoke from his dream and before he could forget it scrawled the word "Cobra" down on a piece of paper. Next morning, he awoke to find the name on his bedside table and knew that this was the name his car would be called.

Besides being a talented driver and car-maker and having the ability to get what he wanted, Shelby was also a natural salesman. He had to be. So far, he only had one car to his name; to make sure others would be built and sold, he needed the help of the automobile media. He began lining up road tests with all the major auto magazines. Such was the response that the first Cobra was barely finished in time for the first test. It didn't have a coat of paint and there was no time to spray it! With the help of some friends, Dean Moon scoured the Cobra's aluminum body until you could see your reflection in it. Grazed knuckles and 20 boxes of scouring pads later, the Cobra was ready to meet the press.

The magazine editors, who thought Cobras were being churned out 19 to the dozen, didn't guess that they were all given the same car to test! It was a clever, if a shade dishonest, ploy. As each magazine's turn came to review the Cobra, Shelby had it painted a different color! Nobody caught on until much later, by which time

Shelby's order book was genuinely full, so nobody minded. The likeable Texan entrepreneur was in fact getting a pat on the back for his ingenuity.

From that moment on, Shelby didn't look back. The Cobra soon became the darling of southern California. Inspired by her Cobra, a young songwriter called Carol Connors wrote a hit single about it, and the title *Hey, Little Cobra* became a catch-phrase with the hot-rod and surfing set. It was all happening out West, but it wouldn't be long before the world would revere this awesome car with the name of one of the deadliest snakes around.

Seventy-five Cobras were built with Ford's 260 cubic-inch engine, to which Shelby also added solid lifters, a tougher camshaft, and a four-barrel carburetor. These little improvements increased output to 260 bhp – or one horsepower per cubic inch. After the first few cars were built, Shelby had to see how it would perform. Once again relying on his gift for salesmanship, he talked his Cobra into the Experimental Production Class in a race dominated by Corvettes at Riverside Raceway in Orange County, California.

Driven by Billy Krause, the bright red Cobra left the Corvettes standing, increasing its lead with every mile. The Corvettes didn't stand a chance of catching the Cobra, which would have won easily had not a stub axle broken at a most inopportune time. Not that anyone wor-

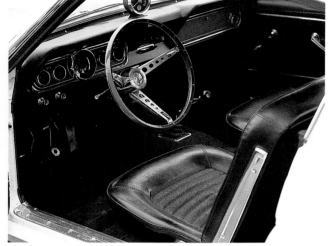

ried, least of all Shelby, who had run his car and proved his point. The Cobra was definitely going to be the car to beat.

Of those early Cobras, no two were exactly alike, as both AC Cars in England and Shelby in California made running improvements to chassis, driving components and engines. Both parties were in constant touch with each other, discussing the merits of various proposed modifications. The entire lightweight, hand-formed aluminum body skin weighed only 50 pounds and was based on the old AC Ace. Shelby suggested rounding out and smoothing the shape which, in accordance with his wishes, AC did. Some say the effect actually reminds them of a Cobra ready to strike, and there certainly is a resemblance. Whether this was intentional doesn't really matter, because the overall effect was very pleasing.

In 1963 Ford enlarged its 260 engine to 289 cubic inches. It came in three sizes, as we already know; a 2 bbl, 200 bhp version; a 4 bbl 225 bhp unit, and finally a 4 bbl, 271 bhp high-performance engine with solid lifters. Shelby chose the latter engine which was also the engine he would use in the Shelby Mustangs, a development still more than two years away. Once they heard that Shelby had this potent new engine, several 260 cid Cobra owners returned with requests for an engine transplant, which Shelby gladly obliged.

THE SNAKE TAKES THEM ON

Ferrari didn't like Shelby; Shelby didn't like Ferrari. The reasons for this animosity aren't quite clear, but that's the way it was. One day, Shelby had promised, he was going to humiliate and crush Ferrari once and for all. With the 289 high-power engine at his disposal, Shelby reckoned his chance had come. He would show that crowd from Maranello, and show them he did. Enzo Ferrari and his creations were trounced on their own turf, right there in Europe in front of crowds brought up to think Ferrari was invincible. How wrong they were.

Drag racing, hill climbs, rallies, road and track racing; whatever the competition was you would find a Cobra – or Cobras – entered. For drag racing, of course, a special Cobra was developed. It was called the Dragonsnake. A few were built by Shelby himself, but the parts were there should individual owners wish to turn their Cobras into dragsters themselves. And quite a few did! Sporting a fiberglass roof, factory and owner-prepared Dragonsnake Cobras dominated the dragster scene until 1967.

Dragonsnakes came well prepared. The engines were the 289 high-power, but came in varying stages of tune, the wildest developing 380 bhp. These engines were blueprinted, balanced and had "Cobra" aluminum valve covers and oil pan. Four Weber carburetors, a special

ABOVE. The heart of the matter. Shelby's re-worked Ford V8 belted out more power than the standard version. Note center bar for added strength. The interior (top) was virtually stock but had Cobra emblems instead of the pony.

camshaft, and much modified heads completed the picture. Much attention was also paid to the suspension – and while the standard axle ratio was 4.89:1, other ratios were also used. The Dragonsnake Cobra's normal run for the drag-strip quarter mile was between 11 and 12 seconds, at speeds of around 116 mph: not bad for Ford's little lightweight V8, especially in 1963.

Back in England, AC was turning out as many body chassis units as possible to keep up with demand. This was about 15, and not more than 20, a week. A visit to AC's Thames Ditton factory revealed that the company had complete records of every Cobra built, including the names of the cars' owners, even second and third owners where possible. It was AC who put together the Le Mans Cobras at Carroll Shelby's request. Two were entered in the 1963 Le Mans, one by AC, the other by a Pittsburgh dealer. AC's car finished the course and came home creditably placed third in its class and seventh overall. It is a moot point really, but it's worth mentioning that Ferrari captured positions one to six overall, a fact that probably didn't go down all that well in Santa Fe Springs!

The competition between Ferrari and Shelby continued apace when full competition Cobras were prepared for the FIA World Manufacturer's Championship in 1963. It was the David and Goliath story of modern times; Ferrari had won the GT class so many times that had there been

laws governing race monopoly, Ferrari would have had a lot of explaining to do! As it was, the Italian marvels had had no competition to speak of until Shelby entered the fray. Not that Cobras acquitted themselves very well in 1963's championship. Apart from Dan Gurney's historic Bridgehampton, N.Y., win, various mechanical ailments plagued Shelby's cars and prevented a serious challenge to Ferrari's superb GTOs.

Things were different in 1964, though. Taking part in all forms of competitive motor sport during 1963 had allowed Shelby and his team to iron out the wrinkles. The cars had proved they were the fastest machines on the track, and with their weak points rectified, the Cobras entered the 1964 season better equipped to break Ferrari's grip on the FIA GT championship.

To do this, Shelby was quick to spot that the successful Ferrari GTOs and Astons were dressed in fairly aerodynamic fastback coupe bodies. The Cobra's was squarish by comparison and was therefore at an immediate disadvantage. Now settled in bigger premises in Venice, California, Shelby-American, as the mercurial little company was called, had the answer to this body problem in a multitalented young man who was pretty adept at car design. His name was Pete Brock.

BROCK'S FASTBACK

Brock designed a fastback coupe body for the Cobra. It

had a longer, lower front which was hinged to expose engine and suspension. The fastback shape was smooth and rounded, tucking in behind the rear wheel arch. The car looked Italian; obviously, Brock was influenced by their design, which might also explain the car's passing resemblance to the famous Ferrari "Breadvan." The first car was put together in the new Venice premises, but the Italian link seems to have spread because, of the six coupes built, five were constructed by Carrozario Gran Sport in Modena, under the supervision of Pete Brock and Shelby-American's chief engineer, Phil Remington.

The coupe's first competition drive was at Daytona, and thus the car was christened the Cobra Daytona Coupe. It was February 16, 1964, the date of the climax of the Daytona Speedweeks: the 12-hour race. Ferrari was there in force, but the lone Daytona Coupe left those gleaming red GTOs in the dust. The car was way out in front and would have won had it not caught fire during a refueling stop. Nevertheless, this lone Shelby put the frighteners on the Ferrari team. A month later, that same Daytona Coupe won the Sebring race. During 1964, Shelby Cobras were successful in many events and were just pipped to the post in the FIA Championships.

By February 1965 Shelby had his six Daytona Coupes ready and waiting. It was third time lucky for the Daytonas, which trounced Ferrari so severely that the Italians went home wondering what had hit them. Shelby

had achieved his ambition. He had beaten everything Europe could produce and had become the first American auto manufacturer to bring home the FIA Championship. Between 1963 and 1965, Cobras picked up 42 international records, scored 17 overall GT class wins and in a total of 27 FIA races set the fastest GT race or GT qualifying lap in 26! Then, on November 6, 1965, Craig Breedlove took a Cobra Daytona to Bonneville. There, he and his co-driver, Bobby Tatroe, drove the Daytona for 12 hours, completing 1,800 miles at an average speed of 150 mph, establishing no fewer than 23 new records along the way!

In Dearborn, Lee Iacocca and his colleagues had been following Shelby's fortunes with much more than a passing interest. After all, Shelby had been using Ford engines exclusively, and Ford's Total Performance program was in full swing. Though indirectly, there was no doubt about it, Shelby-American was doing Ford a considerable amount of good.

Early in 1963 Ford and Ferrari were locked in conference over Ford's possible purchase of the Italian company. If Enzo Ferrari had agreed to the proposed Ford takeover, any future relationship with Shelby-American might have been scuppered. Fortunately for Shelby, Enzo Ferrari figured joining forces with Ford might have an adverse effect on his individual way of doing things; in other words, he would lose his liberty to Dearborn's

*ABOVE AND LEFT. **A rare red and gold example of the GT350H (Hertz) Shelby. Most of the nearly 100 units specially built for Hertz Rent-a-Car were black and gold though other colors were available. GT350H was identical to the standard Shelby GT350. Often Hertz employees would wonder why the rentals would come back in rough condition after a weekend. The truth is that many renters would take the cars to the track and race them. Race on Sunday, return on Monday seemed to be the renters' creed.***

bureaucracy. The answer to Ford's proposal was an emphatic "No."

Disappointed at losing the chance to own the world's most charismatic motoring name, Ford decided to produce its own GT competition car to further company aims at world dominance in motor sport. To this end, Ford created the Special Vehicles Department in June 1963. Visits to Le Mans, England, and Carroll Shelby were next on the agenda; Le Mans because it was *the* race, the international event Ford wanted more than any other to win. In England, Ford's team contracted Eric Broadley, a well-known and respected racing car designer, and John Wyer whom they employed as team manager-cum-driver. Street versions of the GT would be built, and Shelby was given the task of U.S. distribution.

FORD'S GT-40

Of course, the car was the fabulous GT-40. Engineering and design were shared between Ford engineers and Eric Broadley. Ford stylists, with the help of the University of Maryland's wind tunnel, designed the GT-40's overall shape. Construction of finished cars began in late fall 1963 to give enough time for homologation and preparations for the 1964 Le Mans race. The engine in both competition and street cars was the venerable 289, but much modified, especially for competition work.

The whole deal was a bit rushed. Only the bare minimum of testing was completed before Ford launched its answer to world competition racing, dropping it in at the deep end. For these reasons, the GT-40's first season was ignominious to say the least; they were entered in ten races and failed to finish any of them. Nonetheless, Ford was happy it had a potential winner. Eric Broadley, how-

ever, was not and pulled out of the project. Ford then turned to Carroll Shelby and Holman and Moody. To cut a long story short, 427 cubic-inch engines replaced the existing units along with many other modifications. Success still eluded the new GT-40 Mk IIs, mostly through transmission failure. When everything was running right, the big 7-liter GTs left everyone else standing.

In 1966, as we all know, Ford captured the Le Mans crown it so desired. Three GT-40 Mk IIs crossed the finishing line – first, second and third. One of the cars had been prepared by Holman and Moody, while the other two were prepared by Shelby himself (these finished first and second). For the next two seasons, Ford GT-40s dominated competition of endurance races; it shows what can be done when you have the sort of money Ford invested to make its cars successful.

While this was all going on in the competition arena, Ford had decided to give Mustang a performance image. Mustang sales had broken all records for a newly launched car, while the Total Performance program was creating the right sort of image for the big Galaxies as well as the Fairlanes and Falcons. Ford products were making their presence felt on the NASCAR ovals, but there was nothing in Ford's line-up quite like GM's Corvette, which displayed its sporting advantages to the full in the coveted SCCA Championships. The only comparable car Ford had was the Mustang. Pep it up a bit, give it handling suitable to take on Corvette at its own game, and the battle, Ford predicted, could be won. There was only one man available to turn an already good street car into an out-and-out performer...Carroll Shelby, who else? He would create the performance image sorely needed for the pony car.

It was agreed that Shelby-American would have 100 examples ready by January 1, 1965, to enable the Mustang specials to be homologated as a production class racer, in readiness to compete in the upcoming SCCA season. First of all, engineers from Shelby-American built two prototypes out of two Mustang fast-backs. Numerous alterations were made to completely change its boulevard character into a brute-force muscle car. Changes included a fiberglass hood with functional air scoop, Koni shocks, large front anti-sway bar, tougher suspension, a Galaxie rear end, and trailing-arm radius rods. The latter were welded to the frame and rear end housing, thus preventing rear axle hop and spring abnormalities under extreme load.

Under the hood nestled the 289 cid, 271 bhp high-performance engine. Changes included a Cobra aluminum high-rise intake-manifold; finned Cobra cast aluminum valve covers and finned aluminum oilpan; a special Holley center-pivot float carburetor; and steel tube Tri-Y exhaust headers. These were the changes that could be seen, although Shelby's touch also extended inside the engine – special camshaft, for instance. Heavy-duty 11.3-inch Kelsey Hayes ventilated front disk brakes were also a feature, while metallic shoes at the rear improved the

car's stopping power beyond recognition.

To cope with the brutish demands of the engine, an aluminum-cased Borg Warner close-ratio four-speed manual transmission was used. An all-synchromesh box, the Borg Warner had proved itself at drag races when installed in 427 Galaxies and Thunderbolt Fairlanes and was considered ideal for the competition uses to which it would be subjected.

The standard Mustang wheel size of 13 inches was used, but 14-inch diameter wheels were optional. At the beginning of production, 15-inch wheels were also offered but discontinued with the advent of low-profile 14-inch wheels six months later. Yet Shelby's Mustang was given 15-inch, silver-painted wheels scrounged from Ford's station wagon parts bin and shod with Goodyear Blue Dot 7.75x15 tires. The bigger, fatter wheels and tires connected to Detroit Automotive's limited slip differential would prove most effective on the track, where good road grip really does make the difference between winning and losing.

The first 100 cars were all white with black interiors and all references to "Ford" and "Mustang" were deleted from the body. In a blue rocker-panel, a racing stripe carried the car's identity – GT 350 – behind the front wheel opening. Racing-type hood pins were another giveaway to the car's identity and the grille's running horse emblem was relocated to the driver's side. Most, if not all, early GT-350s had 10-inch-wide twin racing stripes running from front to rear, from hood to trunk. This combination of blue striping on white matched America's international racing colors, so there would be no mistake about the GT-350's intentions.

*BELOW LEFT. **Lights are by Lucas, which is popularly known as the "Prince of Darkness" in the U.S.A.***

*BELOW. **Businesslike cockpit is all function, with all controls readily at hand.***

SHELBY-AMERICAN TAKES DELIVERY

Built at Ford's San Jose plant, the 100 blue and white Mustang fastbacks were delivered to Shelby-American for conversion. For those interested in the much-sought 1965-66 Shelby GT-350s, bear in mind that the genuine cars' serial numbers were prefixed "SFM." This was followed by a "5" or "6" which denoted the year of manufacture (1965 or 1966), then an "S" (street) or "R" (race). Apparently the first 25 cars didn't have the "S" designation for one reason or another which has never been fully explained. From number "030" on, however, the letters "S" or "R" appeared when it was decided to differentiate between the street and racing versions.

Five hundred and sixty-two 1965 Shelby GT-350s were built, some in Venice, the rest at Shelby's new, bigger factory, at 6501 West Imperial Highway, a converted aircraft hangar near Los Angeles International Airport.

The cars were marketed through Shelby's established network of Ford dealers who encouraged performance cars and who had been Cobra agents. Demand for the GT-350 was excessive; even the warning that they were "not the cars for everybody" never deterred customers. Hence the reason for opening a new factory to step up production. After all, the Cobra, now with Ford's mighty 427 V8 featuring rear coils instead of the previous leaf openings, was being manufactured in Venice, while there was also the GT-40 program.

The street GT-350s were nearly identical to the racing version, with the major difference being in the engine. As already stated, both used the 289 Hi-Po V8 which, in street trim, pumped out 306 bhp. Racing GTs were developing between 340 and 360 bhp and weighed 300 pounds less at 2,500 pounds compared to 2,800 pounds overall. With this sort of power and weight, the GT-350 would be a formidable contender in the SCCA "B-Production" class where it would compete against small block Corvettes, E-type Jaguars, and the odd Ferrari or Porsche.

From 1965 to 1967, the GT-350 captured the SCCA national class championship. It overwhelmed the "B-Production" class and appeared invincible to all those pitted against it. Corvettes, usually the cars to beat, didn't stand a chance. Just 37 factory-prepared competition GT-350s were put together in San Jose, but all the racing parts were also made available to buyers of the street car.

Genuine, factory-built race cars are easily identifiable by their numbering. Serial numbers on the inner front left fender read as follows: SFMR094 to SFMR108 and SFM5R209 to SFM5R213. The final 13 cars were numbered SFM5R527 to AFM5R539. There were three others, the first race cars, which originally had no numbering, but which were given identities at the end of the model year. These are cars to watch out for, as each model served a specific function. Thus SFM5R001 was a factory team car; SFM5R002 was the factory engineer-

FAR LEFT AND LEFT. **Two more views of the 1967 AC Cobra 427.**

ing car, and SFM5R003 was classed as the prototype and public relations car. Historically, they are priceless, but any of the other competition "R"-suffixed GT-350s must be worth a barrel of money today.

THE GT-350 DRAG

Another competition GT-350 was also built. This was the GT-350 drag car and it came about more by accident than design. A Shelby-American dealer contacted Shelby's PR people in April 1965 with the idea of producing some dragsters out of the GT-350, to follow the successful Dragonsnake Cobras. Well-known race car and engine builder, Bill Stroppe, was given a GT-350 to prepare and evaluate for the purpose. With a watchful eye on the National Hot Rod Association's rule book, 13 drag racing GT-350s (9 in 1965; 4 in 1966) were built.

Modifications included machine-ported cylinder heads and drag valves, while every moving part of the engine was balanced for perfect tolerance. Cure-Ride 90/10 uplock front shocks, Gabriel 50/50 rear shocks, Hurst competition shifter, an NHRA-approved scattershield and a 4.86 rear end ratio made up most of the dragster's package, though individual owners could also add or subtract parts that were NHRA approved. These Stroppe-designed machines held their own on the strip, but it was the SCCA GT-350s that really stole the competition show.

Naturally the automotive press was lining up to road-test the GT-350. "Anyone who tells you it isn't a genuine sportscar is nuts," declared *Car & Driver* breathlessly. The

testers liked its handling, its speed and its brakes. They didn't think it was a lady's car, nor a gentleman's either. A man's car it certainly was, firmly in the tradition of Blower Bentleys and the like.

Through Shelby, Mustang had acquired the performance character Ford wanted. Dramatic though they were, most of the changes were under the skin, so the GT-350 was unmistakably Mustang to look at. Retailing at around $4,547, the GT-350 was a bargain. Where else at that price could an enthusiast pick up a car capable of 0-60 in 6.5 seconds; a top speed of 135 mph, race car handling and an impressive look that stood out from the crowd as a limited production car?

The 1965 GT-350s were advertised as Mustang GT-350s. In 1966 the car became known as the Shelby GT-350, though, apart from the "GT-350" designation, there was no evidence of this on the car itself. There were changes, however. The most noticeable was the addition of a Plexiglass rear quarter window in place of the air extractor louvers. However, functional rear quarter panel side scoops were added, mainly to differentiate 1966 models from 1965. The customer also had four extra colors to choose from: blue, green, black and red with white stripes along the lower sides. White with blue was, of course, continued.

Rear-exit exhausts replaced the side exit system which was considered too noisy by some states' motor vehicle departments as well as a few customers. The "Detroit Locker" rear axle was put on the option list because of

ABOVE. A rare sight indeed. A 427 Cobra being passed by members of the Amish religious sect who can be found in Indiana and Pennsylvania. The Amish eschew all the trappings of modern life and make their living principally as farmers and carpenters using methods subscribed to in the early 1800s. Even their clothes date to the early 19th century. Photography is not allowed, hence the uniqueness of this picture. No doubt some of the younger Amish would be tempted by a car like the Cobra, especially one with such a powerful engine (far right) as the 427.

complaints that it was too loud and given to lurching at lower speeds. Back came the rear seat as an option, which all but 70-odd buyers specified, and the spare returned to the trunk. As the 1966 instrument panel contained five pods including an oil pressure gauge, the Shelby 1965 tachometer/oil pressure option was deleted and replaced by a Cobra 9,000 rpm tachometer mounted atop the instrument panel. On the suspension side, the over-rider traction bars were replaced by under-rider units which could be installed with less problem, while the Koni shocks were relegated to the options book. Standard heavy-duty Ford shock absorbers replaced them. Ford's C-4 automatic transmission became optional, and when this transmission was ordered, an Autolite 595 cfm carburetor was fitted instead of the Holley.

Apparently the first 250 '66 GT-350s were left-over '65s with just the 1966 cosmetic touches added. Serial numbering continued as before, but the "R" for race disappeared, because no competition factory cars were built. Although Shelbys had a good season, all factory cars were the 1965 models, which, apart from the changes described, were essentially the same except perhaps the '66s, which were essentially more Mustang than the 1965 models.

The total production for 1966 was 2,380, including six convertibles built at the end of the run. None of the

six were sold, but were given away to friends and employees of Carroll Shelby. The chances of getting hold of one of those today are virtually nil. Four are known to exist, one has been destroyed, and the other has yet to be located. Another choice Shelby GT-350 collectible is the GT350H; the "H" stands for the Hertz Rent-a-Car Company.

Hertz had switched from GM to Ford for its cars and in consequence had lost the Corvette it offered to those in its Hertz Sportcar Club, a fairly recent and profitable innovation for the company. Shelby-American general manager Peyton Cramer realized the possibilities and lost no time pursuing this little goldmine. First he did a little research and discovered that Hertz had actually produced their own cars back in 1927 and that these cars were painted black with gold trim. Armed with this knowledge, Cramer wooed Hertz with the idea of Shelby GT350s painted black with gold striping; this livery would be exclusive to the rental company. Hertz was suitably impressed, and Cramer thought he could manage at most a 50-car order. He left Hertz, however, quaking with excitement, for the order was not for 50, not for 100, but 1,000 cars! The order accounted for over 40 percent of Shelby production. In four short years, Carroll Shelby had come from nowhere to his peak, a creator of cars idolized then and now.

POWER EXTRA

A special-order option became available for 1966 Shelbys from mid-April of that year. This was a Paxton Supercharger Kit, which once installed would increase horsepower by some 46 percent. Retailing at $670, it was an option that found relatively few buyers – only about 150 dealers installed these units and perhaps a couple were attached by the factory. One hardly dare contemplate the GT-350's potential with a Paxton attached; it was awesome to say the least.

1967 saw the last true Shelby-built GT Mustangs hit the streets. Ford had restyled the Mustang for the first time, its nose had been lengthened by two inches, tread width was given an extra three inches, and the car gained considerable weight. As we are concerned with Shelby and what he did with the basic model, we'll leave a true analysis of the car until the next chapter.

Not that the changes harmed the car all that much in appearance, it was still unmistakably Mustang. The extra weight was something Shelby could have lived without, so Shelby-American designers set to work to lighten the load. On an average 1967 Mustang with the average number of options thrown in, curb weight could be approximately 3,200 pounds. After Shelby's designers had finished with it, the car was 400 pounds lighter.

What they did, with the help of Ford stylist Chuck McHose, was to build a distinctive new front end fabricated entirely out of fiberglass. It was also three inches longer than the standard 1967 Mustang and included a grille unique to Shelby GTs. Some models had two high-beam headlights set in the center of the grille; others had the lights moved to the outer edges, just inside the grille opening, to comply with the laws of certain states. The bumper was stock Mustang minus the bumper guards and the fiberglass front valance had a large cutout permitting a great deal more cooling air to reach the radiator than the standard Mustang did.

As before, the hood was fiberglass, with a large scoop in the center split in two by a leading edge following the hood's center line. Attractive brake cooling scoops replaced the simulated ones on the sides just forward of the rear wheel cutouts and were complemented by interior air extracts on the rear quarter panels. The rear end had a large fiberglass spoiler mated to the fiberglass trunk lid, while quarter panel extensions and the space on either side of the pop-open gas cap was taken up by large horizontal taillights. An interesting feature on the first 1967 Shelbys was a small circular red running light, positioned in the rear end of the quarter panel extractor scoops. This was deleted after the first 200 cars due to production costs and problems involved with wiring them.

Little change was made to the GT-350's running gear apart from the discontinued use of the Tri-Y headers. Instead, Shelby retained Ford's own Hi-Po exhaust manifolds, but the engine still developed 306 bhp as before. However, Shelby went one better than Ford, which now offered the 390 4V big-block "Thunderbird Special" as an option in stock Mustangs. He dropped the big 428 engine into the Shelby and called it the GT-500.

THE NEW 500s

It was actually the 428 Cobra Le Mans engine, used as an alternative to the Cobra 427 when the supply of 427s inexplicably dried up. Without doubt the 427 Cobras, first built in 1965, were everything a Cobra could be and ranked among the fastest production cars in the world. In competition they couldn't be bettered, so it might seem strange that this potent engine wasn't used in the GT-500. The answer is cost (more than twice the 428), sketchy availability, and possibly the problems associated with allowing such an engine to get into inexperienced hands. Anyway, the 428 was powerful enough for the purpose, but it is known that about 45 Shelby GT-500s were built with the 427, going to selected dealers and special-order customers.

Once the public heard about the GT-500, orders came in thick and fast. In fact, the 428 version outsold the 289 GT-350 by two to one. To keep sensitive insurance companies at bay, the GT-500 was advertised as having only 355 bhp, although it was known that it developed far more than that. With dual quad aluminum intake, a pair of Holley 600 carburetors, a high-revving hydraulic valve train and camshaft, the 428 probably generated something nearer 400 bhp.

Both the GT-350 and GT-500 interiors were more or less stock luxury Mustang. A nice touch though – and unique to Shelbys – was a black roll bar with a pair of inertia-reel shoulder harnesses attached. Also different from Ford Mustangs was the real wood steering wheel.

As we said earlier, Carroll Shelby did everything he set out to do. His interest in the Mustang, however, began to cool as 1968 approached, perhaps because the Ford bureaucracy was beginning to call too many of the shots. There were other associated problems too. He hadn't done much racing in 1967; the deaths of drivers who had helped him make Shelby-American what it was – Ken Miles and Dave MacDonald among them – perhaps left too much of a bitter taste in the mouth. Shelby Mustangs would continue, but production and assembly would move to Michigan with Shelby acting as advisor.

It was to prove the end of one of the most colorful and exuberant eras in motoring history. Today few names command the respect and adulation around the world as Carroll Shelby. And 20 years later, people still clamor for Shelby Cobras. At Brooklands, near Weybridge, Surrey, England, a company called Autocraft, set up by Cobra enthusiast Brian Anglis, is recreating Cobras. Built with the blessing of AC Cars (who provided jigs, tools and dies), aluminum-bodied Cobras powered by Ford's 302 V8 are leaving the little factory as fast as they can be produced. Autocraft still builds and sells the only authorized and best Cobra to be found since those halcyon days 30 years ago when Shelby's car was undisputed king.

THESE PAGES. The back of the Cobra is complemented by overall design. This particular car has not much more than 350 miles on it, and its owner has turned down more than $90,000 for it. "Where could I get another like it?" he says.

4
COMPETITION STARTS
THE CHASE

After scoring record sales for a new car, Ford saw no reason to change the Mustang's design as it entered its second year — or to be more precise, its second-and-a-half-year since its first season lasted 18 months. So the Mustang galloped into 1966 with the merest of detail alterations to distinguish it from the year before. For instance, the front grille lost its honeycomb effect and was replaced by an egg-crate design surmounted by thin, chrome horizontal strips. On the Mustang GT (a fastback so-called because the standard model could be ordered with the optional "GT Equipment Group") introduced on Mustang's first anniversary, April 17, 1965, the grille is blacked out. The GT option had chrome horizontal bars flanking the galloping pony, which were deleted on other models.

Other visual changes included a revised simulated air-scoop ahead of the rear wheels. On GT-optional models, 2+2 Mustangs, or those with the Accent Group pin stripe option, the scoop wasn't included. Rocker panel moldings, optional on all but the 1965 2+2, were standard on all '66 models. Some wheel covers and the stylish optional chrome steel wheels were redesigned, and standard wheel size was switched from 13 to 14 inches. Power teams remained unchanged, but now the buyer could specify automatic transmission with the 289 Hi-Po

engine option. The Detroit-Locker 4.30 rear axle was offered as an option, and the Special Handling Package included on Hi-Po powered Mustangs continued as an option on all other models.

Interiors remained much the same, apart from a few upholstery pattern differences, but a major change took place on the instrument panel. The cheaper Falcon-type instrument bezel was dropped in favor of a five-gauge design. A large circular speedometer set in the center and flanked by four smaller dials was a great improvement. Other alterations included a redesigned crashpad and glove compartment door.

There was no let-up in sales for the Mustang, which ended 50,000 units up over the 1965 12-month period, not counting the additional six months that made up the 1965 model year. Mustang had become America's sweetheart and save for the hardly noticed Plymouth Valiant-Barracuda fastback, launched about the same time as the Mustang, there was nothing for Ford to worry about and no competition in sight. Of the three cars in opposition, Corvair Monza, Pontiac GTO, and Barracuda, two were smartly designed compacts while the other was a muscle-bound intermediate. Good cars all (*Car & Driver* had high praise for the performance package optional Barracuda, preferring it overall to the

LEFT AND ABOVE. In 1967, Mustang was restyled primarily to stay ahead of the new competition from GM and Chrysler. That the original pony succeeded goes without saying. The restyling was effective; the car looked little different from the '65/'66 models even though it was. Note the cleaned-up, less awkward front end and more realistic twin simulated rear scoops.

ABOVE. *One of the rarest of all 1967 Mustangs. In 1966, Playboy magazine ordered a few Mustang convertibles for a promotion exercise. In 1967, Ford offered Playboy Pink, which is a Ditzlar color, as a special limited option. Few people took to this hue, but it is known that the models painted this way were convertibles powered by the 289 V8 and equipped with automatic transmission. Except for two, they came with the 390 4V "Thunderbird Special" V8 and a manual four-speed transmission. One car went to Hawaii and has since disappeared, the other to Indiana where it has recently been discovered. Here it is, and while the wheels are after-market (its owner plans to obtain a correct set), this Mustang is truly a unique, one-of-a-kind model. Especially as Ford dropped this color after 1967.*

similarly equipped Mustang), but their combined 1966 sales struggled around the 200,000 mark while Mustang romped home at year's end with a grand total of 607,568 cars built.

Of course, Ford knew that Mustang's days as "Number one in a field of one" – as *MAD* magazine once proudly boasted – were numbered. Power and performance were coming into vogue by the mid-Sixties; anything sporty was gobbled up greedily. And of the differing sporty breeds, it was cars like the Mustang, the pony car concept, that ruled the roost.

MUSTANG RESTYLED

Mindful of the rumblings on the other side of town, Ford set about revising the Mustang to counter whatever threat was to come. What was accomplished was done well without compromising the original theme, even if the stylists fell prey to Detroit's malady of those days – the desire for extra length. Not that the growth of the 1967 models was all that noticeable; the extra inches were added to the nose thus increasing the length from 181.6 inches (the 19641.2 – 1966 model size) to 183.6 inches. The wheelbase remained the same at 108 inches. Largest increase was in the width, which spread from 68.2 to 70.9 inches, though in the sleek, evolutionary restyle, this change wasn't that apparent.

The most noticeable alteration, however, was the front of the 1967 model. Besides the two extra inches, the grille

was considerably larger with the rectangular-mesh insert set farther back. The now-traditional pony still galloped along in its corral, now wider at the bottom in reverse to the '65–'66 design. After a year's absence on standard Mustangs, the chrome flanking bars returned, as did the little horizontal ones, jutting from the top and base of the corral. Overall, the front was more integrated than before, with the side of the grille forming a continuation of the headlight door, whereas before, additional sections with three simulated louvers were usually bolted haphazardly to the sides. Losing those fake louvers was an improvement welcomed by the automotive press, but the simulated rear scoops remained. Actually these were an improvement, if one has to have fakery, over the old. Twin scoops, color-keyed to the body, were set in a deeper, more prominent body side sculpture which came off quite well, losing the awkwardness of the tinsel-like adornment of the earlier design.

Hardtop Mustangs retained much the same roof as before; window glass was unchanged, but the 2+2 was quite different from the 1965-66 model, with the roof sweeping from windshield to tail in an unbroken line, thereby creating a true fastback with the attendant disadvantage applicable to all cars adopting this style – a nearly horizontal, albeit large, back window ideally placed to catch the sun's rays and grow tomatoes on the back shelf. Frivolity aside, however, the overall effect was quite stunning.

Another nice styling touch was the concave rear panel

ABOVE. A 12-louver vent (center) on the side looked more stylish than the previous 5-louver unit, and the horse and bar on the sides had the V8 engine designation set into the bar above the colors (right). The chrome letters that spelled out MUSTANG were longer than in 1966. The taillight assembly (left) looked like three units, but is actually only one; the individual bezels help the illusion.

LEFT. An already good-looking interior was considerably refined for 1967 with an eye on function. Instruments and layout were greatly improved and looked richer. Console and air conditioning were better integrated than before.

housing the three taillights on either side. As on previous models, the lights were in fact one unit per side, cleverly trimmed to look like triple seat sets. Chrome letters spell out the name across the top of the rear panel, while the gas cap, shaped like a wheel knock-off spinner, kept its central location. No additions were made to the number of body types, which remained as hardtop coupe, fastback, and convertible.

These were split into eight different models: hardtop standard, hardtop deluxe, hardtop bench seats, and so on down the line. One interesting variation of the hardtop body style was the Indy Pacesetter Special. This was a limited edition coupe with a unique dual side strip that ran the length of the car. Not much appears to be known about this model, which was more a trim exercise than anything else – or wishful thinking on the part of somebody at Ford, for although the Mustang was the official Indy 500 Pace Car in 1964, it wasn't in 1967.

A minor variation occurred for 1967 only and was part of the GT Equipment Group package. Whereas models with manual transmissions were identified with the letters "GT" within the rocker panel stripe, automatic versions were designated with a "GT-A" emblem in the same location. Instead of the customary pony insignia, all GT cars carried the GT emblem on the gas cap for further identification.

NEW INTERIOR

The interiors were considerably refined for 1967, making an already attractive package even better. A new instrument panel added much to the sporty flavor of the car. Two large circular dials, one for speedometer, the other for tachometer, nestle on either side of the steering column, while three smaller dials are set on the left, right and center of the main pods. The windshield wiper switch sits above the speedometer and the brake warning light is above the tachometer. The steering wheel itself was a new design, featuring a heavily padded central hub flush with the color-keyed rim. Black painted recesses simulate holes in the three chromed, dished spokes. A deluxe steering wheel option has genuine holes drilled through three brushed aluminum spokes, but the rim is simulated wood. (If Shelby could hand out real wooden rims, why not Ford?) All 1967 steering wheels have a horn button at the top of each spoke. And for the first time Mustang buyers could order Ford's nine-position tilt steering column option.

Cars fitted with automatic transmission were blessed with an attractive console extending from the instrument panel to the back of the front seats. At the top is a radio, followed by a vertical sliding door hiding a lighted storage compartment. The overall effect of the console was enhanced by a brushed aluminum finish framed by black strips on either side. Add to this Mustang's luxury interior option consisting of brushed aluminum door panel inserts, brushed aluminum instrument panel bezels, roof console replete with twin map lights and switches, and the buyer had a passenger compartment to rival many other more expensive cars. Keeping all that brushed aluminum clean probably wasn't much fun, though.

Before leaving the interior, mention of the optional Selectaire air conditioning system won't come amiss. In previous years it had hung clumsily from the base of the dashboard like an unfortunate growth. For 1967, Ford designers installed it at the extreme left of the dash (Mustangs without air conditioning had heater/defroster controls set in the same place). Three levers controlled the well-marked functions, and vents were placed below the unit, the same location on the opposite side as well as above the radio.

ABOVE. An interior you can live with for mile after mile. A wide strip of brushed aluminum gives the console sparkle and adds class to an already sleek-looking cockpit.

LEFT. The car emerging from this Ohio peasouper is a 1967 Mustang GT-A, so-called because it has the GT Equipment Group available on any Mustang powered by one of the four V8s available. The "A" suffix denotes that the car is automatic: manual transmission varieties only had the letters GT. The pony, bar and word MUSTANG were deleted if the GT option was specified.

THESE PAGES. *Every so often, a maker of a popular car will show off a special design exercise incorporating innovations that might eventually turn up in a production car. Ford was no exception, as can be seen from this one-off 1967-68 Mustang Mach I show car. Several features from this car eventually found their way into production. The Mach I name arrived in 1969; the hatchback fold-down rear entrance made its debut on the 1974 Mustang II and the styling rear of the doors bears comparison with the 1969-73 sportsroof production models.*

THE FIELD REACTS

The time came for the introduction of the 1967 models, and as expected, a flood of rival pony cars appeared in the showrooms. Chevrolet's Camaro was in the vanguard of the assault, followed by Pontiac, who launched its near-identical twin, the Firebird, at the same time. Chrysler had a newly styled and very attractive-looking Barracuda to throw into the fray, but Ford had a fifth columnist within the opposition. Sister division Lincoln/Mercury introduced the Cougar. Aimed more at the top end of the market, the Cougar was unabashed luxury in sporty guise. A Walter Mitty car if you like, but set up in the right way the Cougar could be a strong performer. Out of almost 140,000 sold in 1967, more than 34,000 were the macho GT and XR-7 models, a healthy indication that there were plenty of red corpuscles at the top end of the market. Following Mustang's lead, all the newcomers had heavy option lists to enable the prospective buyer to choose his own personal car built the way he wanted.

Besides a redesigned body, Mustang was given an additional engine option, the big 380 cubic-inch, 4 bbl Thunderbird Special. Developing 320 bhp, this engine saw service in the Thunderbird, Galaxie and Fairlane.

Understeer was the problem, however, and it is to Ford's credit that they were able to adjust the suspension to cope with the extra power and weight. Road-testers found, if the car was equipped with a good set of tires – and Ford wisely shod 390 Mustangs with F70-14 Firestone Wide-Ovals – the car could tip off 0-60 times in 7.3 seconds and run the quarter in 15, this fully equipped with air conditioning, stereo, electric windows and other extras, as well as turn in a 120-mph top speed. Some said the Mustang in this state of tune wasn't as nifty as the 289, but a competition package was available consisting of stiffer springs, Koni adjustable shocks, limited slip differential, thicker front stabilizer bar, and quicker steering. Dressed up like that, the 390 was a stormer made for the likes of the late Steve McQueen in *Bullitt*, and more than a match for everything the new competition could throw at them. Chevrolet, never one to be upstaged, dropped a 396-cubic-inch engine into the Camaro two months after the car's launch. It was available only in the SS model – the bodywork carrying the "bumblebee" stripe.

With the 390 in tow, Mustang's 1967 engine line-up was increased to five: the standard 200 six; three 289s pushing out 200, 225 and 271 bhp and available with

ABOVE. *1967 Mustangs featured twin simulated scoops set behind the doors in a deeper sculpted recess. Scoops were keyed to the body color.*

RIGHT. *This car has the Interior Decor Group option, featuring brushed aluminum appliques on the doors and the instrument panels.*

a choice of three-speed or four-speed manuals and Cruise-O-Matic. Mindful of the ever-growing safety lobby, all Mustangs came with Ford's "Lifeguard Design Safety Features" including dual hydraulic brakes, impact absorbing steering wheel, safety door latches to keep the doors shut on impact — what happened if the car caught fire, one wonders — padded windshield pillars, seat belts front and rear, and safety instrument panel.

Automobile sales overall dropped by 25 percent in 1967, including Mustang, which had sales down one-fifth over the previous year, though the pony car still out-sold the competition by a wide margin. Add the Cougar's production to the total and Ford's combined market share was almost two to one. A breakdown of the figures is as follows:

Ford Mustang	472,121
Mercury Cougar	150,983
Chevrolet Camaro	220,906
Pontiac Firebird	82,560
Plymouth Barracuda	62,534

Industry sales picked up again in 1968, including Ford, with one exception. Mustang plummeted downward by almost 20 percent. Even so, it still emerged as number one by year's end. The reasons for the drop can be explained: Chrysler had introduced the beautifully redesigned Dodge Charger, while Plymouth stole a march on everybody with the Road Runner. At bargain prices, the spartan Road Runner eschewed luxury options for pure performance with engines going from a 383 to the wild 426 hemi in an intermediate size package. Everything Chrysler touched seemed to be right this year.

It was the same with Ford and GM, too. Ford's Torino, an intermediate powerhouse based on the Fairlane, went on to tear up the NASCAR tracks and develop into the savage Talledega. Customers flocked to the Torino, buying more than 53,000 in 1968. Probably they would have bought Mustangs if this car hadn't come along. Even staid Republican Buick — one tends to think of Buicks being solid and Republican — came out with the wild Wildcat, the GS400. Oldsmobile, Chevrolet, Pontiac all succumbed; only Cadillac remained aloof.

ABOVE. A beautiful 1967 Mustang GT-A in a tranquil lakeside setting.

ABOVE. *A worm's eye view of the 1967 Mustang fastback, and a pretty sight it is, too.*

RIGHT. *A hairy beast if ever there was one – and we don't mean the owner of this special street 'n' strip '68 Mustang. Built specially for the quarter mile, its owner claims the eighth of a mile in seven seconds, the quarter in the lower tens. Power comes from a whopping 428 CJ (Cobra Jet) V8, and the car is alleged to have been one of 50 competition Mustangs built by Ford in mid-1968.*

THE JAVELIN OF AMC

Then the one company nobody thought of ever getting into muscle cars joined the bandwagon. American Motors (AMC), makers of sensible cars since swallowed up by Chrysler Corporation, popped up and surprised everyone with the Javelin. The size of the Cougar but aimed to compete with Mustang and Camaro, the Javelin had the power to run with the new musclebound herd. AMC even went racing, taking on the big boys in SCCA's Trans-Am championships. The Javelins didn't win in '68 or '69, though Camaro did, much to Mustang's chagrin. In 1970 Mustang just beat Javelin to the winning post, but Javelin finally succeeded in 1971.

The Javelin was an attractive car and the buyers thought so, too. 58,462 Javelins found homes in 1968, much to AMC's delight. "Nattily handsome... altogether appealing," said *Automobile Quarterly*. AMC was pleased with Javelin's success, so much so they put a little gilding on the lily and in mid-1968 came out with the pretty little AMX. Actually a truncated Javelin (stylist Richard Teague removed 12 inches from its chassis), Teague managed to make the AMX look like a different car. Which it was. All sheet metal was incompatible with AMX's bigger brother. Another headache for Mustang, as if it wasn't suffering enough.

Muscle cars, Rambos on wheels (much more appetizing than the human version), were signs of the times in psychedelic 1968. Flower power, Timothy Leary, the Beatles, Mayor Daley and Robert Kennedy's assassination: somehow the climate seemed tailor-made for a motoring revolution that lasted only a few short years but left its mark. The likelihood is, if it wasn't for the Mustang, the muscle car might never have been.

But the Mustang was a car to last. It had captured the world's fancy, and for two and a half years, it was out on its own. By 1968, however, it was being attacked from all sides and though it led, its sales position had been eroded by the sprightly new contenders, chiefly the Camaro, which was in second place and was still increasing in sales.

The changes to the 1968 Mustang were minimal, and it was a particularly sharp-eyed individual who could spot the differences over the 1967 models. The giveaway was the front and rear fender mounted sidelight/indicator units required by Federal law. Other safety features were added to the interior, though many were carried over from 1967, when Ford pre-empted the Government by installing many of the requirements itself. The new additions were self-locking folding seats, shoulder belts, windshield-mounted rear-view mirror, energy-absorbing seat backs, and safety designed control knobs.

What exterior modifications there were included the removal of the chrome bars attached to the running horse corral on the grille. The corral and horse were smaller for '68, and the mesh grille had a thin chrome strip following the grille's outline as a sort of frame. Bumper guards were no longer standard and became another number on the option sheet. Gone, too, were the letters spelling out "Ford" across the front of the hood. The block letters used for the word "Mustang" behind the horse and bar fender emblem were changed to script. For the first time, the windshield curvature was slightly altered and side windows were curved. A new gas cap had a running horse and corral, similar to the one on the grille, and had only two "knock off" blades instead of three as in the '67. Still simulated but now of simpler design was the rear quarter panel scoop. A vertical chrome motif with black paint inside the front leading edge replaced the previous years' twin scoops.

BELOW. First it was the 1940 Continental, then the 1955-57 T-Bird; the '56 Continental Mk II, the '55, '59 and '64 Fords. When Ford designs an attractive car, it takes some beating. Much the same can be said of the 1967 Mustang, shown here in convertible form. Today's Ford products carry on the tradition with undoubtedly the best looking series of cars to be seen in years.

FAR LEFT AND LEFT. Mustang's pony and bar pop up everywhere. Here it is on the 1967 steering wheel hub, heavily padded for safety. Ford pre-empted Federal legislation by adding many safety items in 1967, including an impact absorbing steering wheel, a safety inspired instrument panel and controls.

BELOW. *Fat rear slicks and special wheels mean this '67 quarter miler is a mean machine indeed.*

THE LIMITED EDITIONS

The number of bodystyles remained as before, but the number of models increased to 10. Some interesting model variations appeared in 1968. Taking advantage of Mustang's enormous popularity in California, where one in every five built was sold, Ford produced a limited edition "California Special." Unavailable anywhere else, this exclusive Mustang was available in hardtop coupe form only and was distinguished by a Shelby-style grille complete with Lucas fog lamps. More Shelby spin-offs included taillights, fiberglass rear scoops (non-functional in the Special's case) and fiberglass rear deck lid. Mustang's optional louvered hood was standard on the GT/CS (GT/California Special) and held down by twist-type hood locks. A special side stripe flowed from the headlight caps right down the middle of the car's side to the rear scoop with the letters "GT/CS" etched into the stripe. Standard engine was the six, but all V8s and other Mustang equipment were options, in common with other models.

Colorado also got its own special limited edition. It was identical to the California Special with the exception of the name which identified the car as the "High Country Special." A shield decal has a gold horse galloping against a blue sky with a jagged gold line representing the Colorado mountains with the words "High Country Special '68" picked out in gold. Both cars were available for one year only and are naturally very sought-after models today.

LEFT AND BELOW LEFT. **What better way to enjoy a sunny, warm fall day than a country cruise in your 1967 convertible? It looks at home parked with the top up beside a field of corn.**

Keeping with the specials for the moment, it's worth mentioning the Mustangs that were exported overseas. Models destined for Europe were generally fitted with stiffer suspension to cope with the many smaller, winding roads to be found. In Britain, strong headlights were fitted to comply with lighting regulations, which permit twice as much candlepower as the U.S. This would also apply in Europe. An interesting anomaly were the Mustangs exported to Germany. Because the word "Mustang" was already copyrighted for another product, no German-bound Mustangs were named as such. Instead, they were called Ford T-5s and given T-5 emblems where "Mustang" used to be. T-5, as you will recall, was the Mustang code-name in the very beginning.

Due to Federal government-mandated emissions standards taking effect, there was a bit of juggling around with the choice of engines in 1968. Seven were offered, but some were detuned. The basic six dropped five horsepower to 115 bhp, and its compression ratio was lowered from 9.2:1 to 8.8:1. Only one 289 remained, the 2 bbl with a similar compression ratio drop and horsepower down from 200 to 195. Instead of the mid-performance 289, a 302 cid unit was put in its place, although it was really the bored-out 289. Called the Challenger Special, the 4 bbl engine put out 230 bhp.

With the excellent 289 Hi-Po gone, the 390 stepped into its shoes as the premier powerhouse. Horsepower climbed to 335. Floating caliper front disk brakes were a mandatory option with this unit, although the buyer paid more for the privilege.

THESE PAGES. *Both the High Country Special (above) and the California Special (right) were virtual twins, sharing Mustang Shelby items such as taillights, grille, scoops and hood locks. The only difference was the trim/decal identity. Like the GT-A, both Specials were in production for one season only.*

RIGHT. *Big engines were the order of the day in '68, and Ford began to shoehorn 390 4V and 428 CJs under Mustang's hood to keep abreast – and ahead – of the competition.*

ABOVE. *Ford's biggest fear was Chevrolet's Camaro, launched in September 1966 as a 1967 model. A wide choice of engines, handling, and trim options put it firmly in Mustang's field. Nonetheless, Mustang held onto first place by a considerable margin. Equipped with a 396 cid V8 like this '68 model, the Camaro was no slouch on either street or strip.*

UPPING THE STAKES

A horsepower race of frightening intensity now had Detroit in its grip. Chrysler was chucking mighty 440 wedge and 426 hemis into anything on wheels if customers requested them. GM was playing around with 425s and 427s, and Ford upped the pony-car ante by offering – at $755 for the pleasure – its mighty 427 wedge, first developed for racing and for powering Galaxie 500XLs, in the Mustang. This was a huge, hefty lump to lever into Mustang's engine bay, but the necessary modifications had already been carried out for the 390 a year earlier.

The 427 wedge, introduced in 1964, had successfully

powered bigger Fords as well as performing with distinction on the racetrack. It had five main bearings with the middle three crossbolted for additional strength. Torque was 460 ft/lbs at 3,200 rpm, an incredible amount. Compression was 10.9:1 and horsepower was rated at 390 gross. An awesome engine in a lightweight car equipped with decent suspension and brakes, that was the 427 Mustang. Yet for some reason it didn't sell all that well. Possibly Ford, wary of the clamoring safety lobby, didn't give it enough exposure, because the performance-minded didn't appear aware of this engine's potential.

So Ford dispensed with it entirely after 1968; a great shame perhaps. It would have been even sadder had not Ford put another challenge on the table. On April 1, 1968, Ford introduced the fire-eating Cobra Jet Mustang equipped with a new 428 Cobra Jet V8. This was the ultimate king of the road in 1968, Mustang's right to stand top of the pile. No mistakes this time; Ford let everybody know that a new monster had arrived and the performance enthusiasts were quick on the uptake.

In fact, the Cobra Jet's compression ratio was lower than the 427 at 10.5:1; its bore was 4.130 compared to 4.236 and its stroke was 3.984 versus 3.781. Therefore its volume was much the same as the 427, but its longer stroke and lower compression made for a more docile unit on the street. The cylinder heads, however, had bigger ports than the 427 racing heads, and very large intake and exhaust valves combined to make the 428 CJ a tougher proposition altogether. Unlike the 427, which came only with automatic transmission, the 428 CJ could be had with a four-speed manual as well.

Referred to as a 1968½ model due to its late introduction, the Cobra Jet Mustang was available in fastback form only. It was easily identified from the rest of the herd because it had grille fog lights, a wide, flat black hood stripe, and was the first production Mustang to feature a functional hood airscoop. A "GT" emblem replaced the traditional horse behind the front wheel arches, and the side sculpturing was accented by a stripe running the car's entire length. Staggered rear shocks came on all four-speed manual cars as did an 8,000 rpm tachometer, the latter optional on automatics. The Cobra Jet was the most powerful production Mustang up to that time, yet it didn't exactly meet with Lee Iacocca's approval. Times were changing; Mustang's original concept was being irrevocably changed in favor of "bigger is better."

Mustang production and other pony cars for 1968:

Mustang	317,404
Camaro	235,151
Cougar	113,726
Firebird	100,000 (an approximation based on available figures)
Barracuda	45,412
Javelin	56,462

MUSTANG WITHOUT IACOCCA

After the Mustang's initial runaway success, Henry Ford II pushed Iacocca upstairs to the executive "Glass House" (a term by which Ford employees referred to the head offices), where he became vice-president of Ford's entire car and truck group. This meant he had responsibility for much else besides the Ford Division and obviously could no longer be as intimately involved with Mustang's fortunes as he had been before. Perhaps his attention was diverted to the Lincoln/Mercury Division and the luxurious but ailing Lincoln itself was taking up too much of his time.

It was he who suggested putting a Rolls-Royce type grille on the Continental Mark II. It made its debut in 1968, and such was its appeal that it outsold Cadillac's front-wheel-drive Eldorado. And to outsell Cadillac, any model of Cadillac, was – and still is – the true mark of success.

A gentleman by the name of Arjoy Miller was Ford corporate president in 1968. He conducted his responsibilities quietly and efficiently. Then Henry Ford II heard rum-

LEFT AND BELOW LEFT. Mustangs faced stiff opposition from rival pony cars and a host of muscle cars. One of the best was Dodge's restyled Charger with engine options running from the standard 318 V8 to the ferocious 425 cid hemi. The most talked-about was the "plain-Jane" Plymouth Road Runner. This was a bargain basement muscle car designed to handle and go fast without luxury frills to impede its phenomenal performance. The car shown is a '69 model. Enthusiasts will fondly remember its Road Runner cartoon emblem and "Beep! Beep!" horn.

*THIS PAGE. **Perpahs the most desirable Mustang of all, the 1969 Boss 429. Only 1,300 of this potent machine were built between 1969 and 1970 to homologate the semi-hemispherical V8 built purely for racing. Each car equipped with this engine has a tell-tale NASCAR tag on the lower edge of the driver's door and 429 stamped on the engine's rocker covers.***

blings from GM: Simon "Bunkie" Knudsen, the man who put power back into Pontiac, wanted to get out of what he thought was becoming a dead-end position. Henry Ford wanted this man, a man whose father had once been president of GM. What a catch, what a coup. He went after Knudsen.

Arjoy Miller suddenly found himself promoted to vice-chairman of the Ford empire. Everybody thought the vacant position of president would surely go to Iacocca. It

didn't. Ford's new president was Bunkie Knudsen. Henry Ford was pleased; that neat piece of recruitment of a top GM executive gave to Ford a man who knew the inner workings of what made the General tick. Yes, Henry Ford was pleased. Problem was, the rest of Ford's team wasn't quite so ecstatic.

One of the first things Knudsen did was to fatten up the Mustang. To help him, he had talked top GM stylist Larry Shinoda into joining Ford as head of the Special Design

LEFT. Another powerhouse was the Plymouth GTX. Essentially a Road Runner with luxury as well as performance, this 1969 model boasts a 440 six-pack under the hood.

Center. Shinoda was an excellent designer whose influence was soon apparent on Ford styling. He created the fastback Torino Cobra, a wild 428-powered intermediate which, in various guises, would become the scourge of the NASCAR ovals – until Chrysler popped up with the ultimate racers, the Dodge Daytona and Plymouth Superbird. Events were happening fast at Ford, so fast that the Knudsen/Shinoda influence began to show on the 1969 Mustangs, even though the basic design had been laid down before Shinoda arrived.

Having grown two inches in 1967, Mustang stretched a further four in 1969 bringing its total overall length to 187.4. Most of this extra length was at the front. More width was also added, bringing it from 70.9 inches to 71.3. The wheelbase remained as before, but the long-hood, short-deck theme was heavily accentuated, a styling ploy so common by now that it was found on everything from Continentals to Corvettes, Checker taxi-cabs being the exception to the rule, though as Checker never changed anyway, it didn't really count.

THE NEW MODELS

Although drifting away from what Iacocca thought a sporty car should be, the 1969 Mustang was an attractive-looking machine. Ten models were offered in the usual three bodystyles: fastback, hardtop, and convertible. Ford decided the term "fastback" was passe, so the bodystyle was renamed "sportsroof." An imaginative term, but at the end of the day it was still a fastback, whatever you called it.

Whichever way you looked at it, the Mustang was a different car. From its dark gray rectangular mesh plastic grille (all metal before 1969) to its smoother, non-sculp-

tured sides, the Mustang had created itself a new image. No longer the sassy character that endeared millions: now the look was deadly serious, mean and moody. Apart from the triple taillight clusters, little remained of Iacocca's brainchild. It had grown up to become a sullen teenager, depending of course on your point of view. If one forgets what went before, the '69 Mustang was a striking automobile, still better-looking than the rest of the crowd. It had some nice touches, including the racy-looking, swept-back headlight housings and the gentle "V" shaping of the front. The stylists didn't seem sure where they should hang the fake rear quarter panel scoops, so they compromised. On convertibles and hardtops, a rear facing exhaust vent was positioned ahead of the rear wheel arch, and on sportsroof models a realistic-looking scoop is fared into the rear quarter panel just behind the door handle.

The rearward slope of the windshield was more pronounced and the glass area increased in size. Hardtop, sportsroof, and convertible roofs where redesigned; the hardtop's "C" pillars were made wider, forming a tunnel effect for the rear window. Side louvers on the sportsroof were replaced by a simple round emblem with the running horse encased within. The roof itself was beautifully styled, a graceful rearward sweep flowing into the kicked-up rear deck. Tinted rear glass was standard on the sportsroof, no doubt necessitated by its almost horizontal position.

Front standard bucket seats now included headrests in compliance with Federal safety standards, though sportier high-back buckets were an option. Most of the 1969 interior was completely redesigned, with the emphasis on safety and style; twin hoods, thickly padded instruments

THIS PAGE. **Car & Driver** thought the 1969 Boss 302 was the best of all Mustangs, with handling that outclassed Shelbys and Mach Is. The Boss 302 was good because it had two tasks – to take on the Camaro Z-28 threat and to qualify it for the SCCA Trans-Am race series. Like the 429, the engine was built for racing, and like the 429, it was available only for two seasons. This was the 1969 example.

and glove compartment, the design dipping in the middle to form the radio/heater control panel. The instruments were deeply recessed in four pods: two larger ones in the center served as speedometer, fuel gauge and temperature gauge. Warning lights for brakes and seat belt reminder took up the left and right sections of the fuel temperature pod. A running horse served as a high-beam warning indicator below the 12 o'clock position on the speedometer. An alternator gauge took up outer left and right pods in that order. On optional instrument panels, a tachometer took the place of the fuel/temperature/warning light pod, with the fuel gauge replacing the alternator. Both alternator and oil pressure were relegated to warning lights on the tachometer's lower perimeter.

The stock steering wheel was a two-spoke design, but a three-spoke Rim-Blow – so-called because it had a horn switch set into the inner rim – with simulated wood-grain rim was an option. Standard upholstery had vertical pleats, but the high-back buckets had a horizontal pattern. The door panels were all new in two different styles, but all had a small pony and tricolor bar motif affixed just below the rim.

Whatever the model, however, one policy didn't change through the years, and that was the choice of a staggering range of options to enable the buyer to equip his car the way he wanted it. It was an idea copied by everyone else, for the very good reason that it worked so well. Mustang for 1969 had two Interior Decor Groups; the GT Equipment Group (which was in its final year); an Exterior Decor Group; and a Visibility Group, as well as the choice of eight engine variations, three transmissions, and a host of other items. Also added to this impressive array were four new special models: the Mach I, Boss 429, Boss 302, and the luxury Grandé.

For engine variations, the 200 six was still Mustang's base engine, though it got company in 1969. For $39 extra, six-cylinder buyers could order a 250 cid, 155 bhp six with a little more zip. Rumor had it that Ford was working on a fuel-injected version, as well as designing a hop-up kit for the 250, but neither idea materialized.

The famous 289 had gone to be replaced by the 302 2V engine, rated at 220 bhp as the base V8. Then came a 351 2V and 351 4V. These were new for 1969, albeit based on the 289/302 block. Modifications, like a different combustion chamber, turned it into a powerful unit nobody would be ashamed of. But the real monster was the 428 Cobra-Jet, and an out-and-out performance Mustang was designed especially for it.

LEFT. *Wherever a Boss 429 appears, it draws attention, sometimes of an unwelcome kind...*

ABOVE. *Duesenberg's "Power of the hour" slogan would be an appropriate description for the Boss of Bosses – the 429.*

PRESENTING THE MACH I

As cars go, particularly sporty cars, the Mach I equipped with the Cobra-Jet engine was a machine to be treated with respect. It was one of the fastest production cars in the world with an engine originally designed by Ford's Light Vehicle Powertrain Department, headed by Tom Feaheney for drag racing. For use in the Mach I, engineer Matt Donner placed one rear shock absorber behind the axle and the other in front of it to prevent wheel hop. Simple but effective, this quite unoriginal idea worked very well.

As for the automotive press, they waxed lyrical over the Mach I, which is hardly surprising when *Hot Rod* magazine in its test managed 0-60 in 5.9 seconds; then a quarter-mile dash in 13.56 seconds at 106.64 mph. *Car Life* bettered the 0-60 time, running through in 5.5 seconds, though its quarter-mile run of 13.90 seconds at 103.32 wasn't quite as good. Who cared: *Car Life* said it was the fastest standard passenger car they had ever tested, that it was, "A superb road car, stable at speed, tenacious on corners, with surplus power and brakes for any road situation." What more could be said; nearly

every auto journal was coming to the same conclusion. The Mach I was, and remains, one helluva car.

Breathing heavily over the Mach I is quite understandable, especially if you own one. However, it should not be forgotten that Mustang also had the Boss 302 in its stable. If any Mustang showed true Shinoda influence, the Boss 302 was getting close. Designed primarily to compete against Camaros in SCCA's Trans-Am series, Shinoda added front and rear spoilers, the latter adjustable. Another touch was the flat black rear-window slats, a styling gimmick that did nothing to help performance even if it did look good.

Never mind the slats — nobody had to have them if they didn't want to — it was the car itself, built purely to race, that was so interesting. One thousand units had to be made to qualify the 302 for the Trans-Am series. In fact, Ford put together 1,934 in 1969, not exactly a record-breaking number bearing in mind the way Mustangs normally poured out of the factories. Obviously Ford wasn't interested in mass-marketing the 302 when the Mach I was there as the heady performance machine. False economy perhaps, because the Boss 302, equipped with competition suspension consisting of staggered rear shocks, thicker front anti-roll bar and stiffened springs coupled with a quick 16:1 steering ratio, was infinitely a better-balanced car. Weight distribution

of 55.7 percent in the case of the Mach I obviously helped. *Car & Driver* magazine, never as enamored of the 428 CJ Mach I as other journals, called the Boss 302 the "Best Mustang yet and that includes all of the Shelbys and Mach Is."

The 302 engine was conservatively rated at 290 bhp gross, though it was estimated that its actual power was nearer 400. Hardly surprising when one considers the engine used what was known as "Cleveland" heads, possessing huge intake and exhaust valves, aluminum high-rise manifold, Holley 4 bbl carburetor, forged crankshaft, and special pistons. Actually the Cleveland heads were scheduled for 1970 production, but their breathing properties were superior to equivalent 1969 heads and convinced Ford to use them on the mid-1969 Boss.

Considering its size compared to the 428 CJ, the 302 was no chicken. It could race to 60 in 6.9 seconds and hit the quarter in 14.85 seconds at 96.15 mph. Not as quick as a Camaro Z-28 with a similar-size engine, it took exactly the same time to reach the quarter, but its trap speed was just over 101 mph. The proof, however, is in the driving, and Camaro proved that, with an impressive Trans-Am season capturing the crown for the second year running. Nonetheless, Mustang's Boss 302 won a couple of the 12 races in convincing style, serving warning to Chevrolet that this was only the beginning.

*ABOVE. **The 1969 Mach I with yet another powerhouse engine, in this case, the 428 CJ Ram-Air.***

ABOVE LEFT AND LEFT. Coming or going, the 1969 Boss 429 and Boss 302 turn any fan's head. Rear sports slats and spoiler were options. The 302 could hit 60 in 6 seconds, the Boss 429 almost as fast if you could afford its fuel consumption.

INSET ABOVE. 1969 was the last year for the Mustang GT Equipment Group options, as new models like the Mach I and luxury Grandé came with option packages as standard.

THIS PAGE. *Not all Machs had the 428 CJ – most came with the 351 cid V8. The interior of the sportsroof – the only body style for Mach Is – inclined toward luxury with phony wood everywhere. Taillights were three separate units framed by chrome bezels.*

THE WILD BOSS 429

The wildest of the ponies, be they Mustangs, Camaros or Javelins, had to be the very limited production Boss 429. This was an engine designed and built almost exclusively for the racetrack. It was quite unlike any other engine built by Ford. Conceived to do battle with the Dodge/Plymouth on NASCAR'S super ovals for a chance to win the coveted Grand National Championship, Ford had to build 500 to be sold to the public to satisfy NASCAR's homologation rules. It didn't matter what car the engine was put into as long as the required number of engines were sold. With this in mind, Ford chose the Mustang sportsroof body to further the pony-car's performance image.

What Ford's engineers did was to take the 429 thin-wall block used in the Thunderbird and full-size Fords, then added aluminum semi-hemispherical combustion chambers. A "twisted hemi" some called it. This configuration allowed for superior breathing, for the ports, intake passages, and the oval exhaust valves were gigantic. The valves themselves were set across from each other to form a crossflow cylinder head. A cast aluminum manifold mounted a single four-barrel Holley carburetor, while the valve covers themselves were designed for easy removal, as were the hemi-style plug locations. If only engineers would think of ease of maintenance today!

Everything underneath was heavy duty. It had to be, bearing in mind the engine size. To facilitate mounting into the Mustang, the engineers had to move the front suspension outboard an inch to allow the upper A-arm pivot and spring tower to clear the valve covers. While they were working on this, it was decided to lower the inside attachment point an inch to enhance front-end geometry. As for the suspension itself, it derived from the Mach I competition set-up, but with ultraheavy-duty Gabriel shocks, fat front and rear stabilizer bars, and staggered rear shocks.

The body was much the same as the Boss 302 with the addition of the largest functional hoodscoop ever to grace a Mustang hood. A choice of six single body colors were offered: black, white, red, blue, maroon and black jade. The only outward sign to denote the car's potential was a Boss 429 decal mounted on the front fenders behind the wheel openings. The tough four-speed manual transmission was Ford-built and floor-mounted, in an interior bordering on the luxurious.

Road tests found the street version Boss 429 slower in every respect when compared to a 428 Mach I. It took the 0-60 in 7.1 seconds and the standing quarter in 14.90 at a speed of 102.85 mph. With a curb weight of 3,560 pounds compared to the Mach's 3,420, this is understandable, but this engine was primarily designed for ultra-high-speed cruising at the NASCAR tracks. On

BELOW. Another new model for '69 was the Grandé. Available as a hardtop only, the Grandé had a vinyl roof in keeping with its luxury image. Standard engine was the 200 cid six, and you couldn't specify handling suspension even if you opted for the bigger engine like the 351. Fifty-five pounds of extra sound insulation went into the Grandé, which had unique hopsack cloth seat inserts and fairly good imitation teakwood trim. (Photo courtesy Jim Smart, Dobbs Publications.)

LEFT. Descended from the 1962 302 engine, the 351 became Mustang's staple diet from 1969 through 1973. This 1970 convertible is an attractive car.

BELOW. In 1970 Boss 429 was in its last year. Even though it wasn't as fast and didn't handle as well as the Boss 302, the 429 is a brute-force car that attracts a lot of collector dollars these days.

the other hand, it is said that Ford guaranteed the quarter mile in 13 seconds. If this is the case, then the 429 obviously had to be set up right to do it. Certainly, none of the few magazines who tested the 429 approached 13 seconds, possibly because the car was tuned for the street.

THE LUXURY MUSTANG

Going from one extreme to the other was the Grandé. Available in hardtop form only, the Grandé was the soft-shoe-shuffle Mustang for the luxury boulevard set. Its interior came with many luxury options as standard and had simulated wood all over the place. An additional 55 pounds of sound insulation came with the car along with much softer spring settings, though there was nothing to stop buyers from choosing big-block engines and stiff suspension for it. The base engine was the ubiquitous six, and for the extra $230 the customer paid over the standard Mustang, the Grandé was quite a chintzy machine. Of course there was, as with all Mustangs, an option list a mile long. Unique to the Grandé were special bucket seats with hopsack cloth inserts as well as a vinyl roof.

Even with additional special models and massive performance, Mustang sales slid even further down the scale. Only 299,824 were produced in 1969, though this still kept ahead of Camaro's growing total of 234,095. Camaro had a lot going for it in '69: it won the Trans-Am Championship as well as being selected as the Indy 500 Pace Car, which is more than can be said for the Barracuda, which had sales declining to 32,987.

Despite optimism in the Ford camp, if anything, 1970 was Mustang's worst year yet. Only 190,727 were produced, though Ford could take small comfort in the knowl-

THESE PAGES. A 1970 Mach I with optional 351 4V V8. Large die-cast Mach I lettering adorns the side below the Mustang script, while the "Shaker" is a functional option, but standard on 428-equipped Machs.

edge that all other pony-car sales were down, too, including those of the Camaro at 124,899, thus allowing Mustang to stay on the top rung. Possibly the major reasons for the sales decline were the increased Federal regulations, a public tiring of sports and muscle cars and their subsequent high insurance rates, and a general apathy among consumers, a condition auto manufacturers have to put up with every ten years or so.

One of the results of the decline was that Bunkie Knudsen had gone. After 19 months Henry Ford fired him. "Things just didn't work out," replied Ford vaguely when asked why. There was much relief and rejoicing among Ford's staff, however, when they heard the news. Even Iacocca was quietly pleased, for he knew a GM-trained man could not fit into Ford's entirely different way of doing things. Apparently Knudsen tried to be too familiar with Henry Ford, and if there was anything you didn't do, it was to do the "old pals" act with him. A year later

on December 10, 1970, Lee Iacocca finally became president of the world's second-largest automobile company. And, as everybody agreed, it was about time, too.

FROM '69 TO '70

The 1970 Mustangs changed little in appearance over the 1969 models. Immediate identity clues can be found at the front where the headlights were reduced from four to two, with the other lights replaced by a cap containing twin horizontal simulated airscoops. Side marker lights are vertical in the front and positioned higher on the fenders. Both the optional rear-window slats and rear deck spoiler, an exclusive on the '69 Boss 302, were made available for all Mustang models.

All model types continued in production as before, the exciting Boss 302 and Boss 429 returning for another year. A single season special also appeared in 1970. This was a 428CJ Mach I variant called "Twister

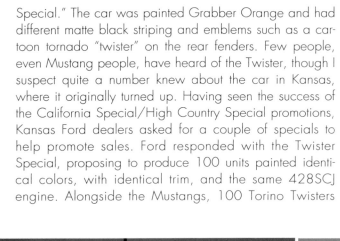

Special." The car was painted Grabber Orange and had different matte black striping and emblems such as a cartoon tornado "twister" on the rear fenders. Few people, even Mustang people, have heard of the Twister, though I suspect quite a number knew about the car in Kansas, where it originally turned up. Having seen the success of the California Special/High Country Special promotions, Kansas Ford dealers asked for a couple of specials to help promote sales. Ford responded with the Twister Special, proposing to produce 100 units painted identical colors, with identical trim, and the same 428SCJ engine. Alongside the Mustangs, 100 Torino Twisters

were also to be built, but with the powerful 429SCJ.

All Twisters got Traction-Lok limited slip differentials, and they were all meant to be the same. But the best-laid plans often go awry, and they did in the Twister's case. Halfway through the run, Ford ran out of 428 engines, so half the cars ended up with the 351 Cleveland V8. Nine of the 351 powered cars had four-speed manual transmissions; the rest were automatics. Of the remaining Twisters with the 428 engine, 24 had the four-speed manual, 24 the automatic. Built on the Mach I line, all 96 Twisters – for some reason, the final four were never built – have consecutive VIN numbers. And nobody's telling

what the numbers are to prevent fake Twisters from suddenly turning up. One fake has been discovered by the Twister Special Club, run by Terry Fritts. It comes from Texas and can be spotted by the VIN number which begins 190. Real Twisters have quite different numbers, and 190 doesn't start any of them.

At the time of writing, three Twisters reside in California, including the car shown here. Of the 96 built, 46 have been found, with a further four known to have been destroyed. Of the 46, very few have been completely restored. Current values for a restored car run around $50,000 for a 428, $35,000 for the 351. Compared to the prices of some other collectors' cars from the same period, these cars are still quite a bargain for what they represent.

Mustangs did well at the track, winning back the SCCA Trans-Am Championship they had lost in 1968. New and very much in the performance mode, Ford offered a Hurst competition gear-shift with T-handle. It is interesting to note that Ford's 429 V8 powered cars trounced Chrysler products on NASCAR tracks in 1968 until late in '69, when Dodge showed up with the lethal Daytona. Plymouth offered the ultimate racer in 1970 with the Superbird. Between them, these "winged warriors" extacted sweet revenge.on Ford, whose racing prowess went into decline after 1969.

An interesting aside was the prices of these cars. In 1964 a base six-cylinder Mustang sold for about $2,400; in 1970 the same basic car listed for $2,700, only $300 more. A 1970 V8 convertible was only $3,126 and only when the buyer reached the Boss 429 did the price move appreciably upward. Even then, equipped with all necessary performance options, a $4,850 sticker price was nothing, considering what the dollars bought.

Ford Division general manager John Naughton had said the Seventies' Mustangs would emphasize performance. It was, he said, going to be the "sizzlin' Seventies." Someone, somewhere was out of touch, for as 1970 closed, Ford abandoned factory participation in competition.

Buyers now wanted more room, luxury, size; so the new, restyled 1971 Mustangs were right on cue. Longer, lower, wider, this was Larry Shinoda's legacy. He had come to Ford with Bunkie Knudsen and he left Ford with Bunkie Knudsen, though not before laying down the designs for the biggest Mustang ever. Iacocca described it as a "fat pig," but there wasn't much he could do about it. In 1969 he gathered those who had helped him with the original car. He and Hal Sperlich flew to Italy to visit Alejandro de Tomaso, head of Ghia Studios in Turin. By early 1970, Ford had de Tomaso's prototype for what was to become the 1974 Mustang II.

There was little to compare between the 1971 Mustang and what had gone before. Length had increased 2.1 inches to 189.5 inches overall, width was up by 2.4 inches and was now approaching sedan dimensions at 74.1 inches. Height dropped an inch on convertibles, slightly less on hardtops and sportsroofs, but the wheelbase increased for the first time from 108 to

THESE PAGES. *The sleek 1973 351 Ram Air coupe and the convertible.*

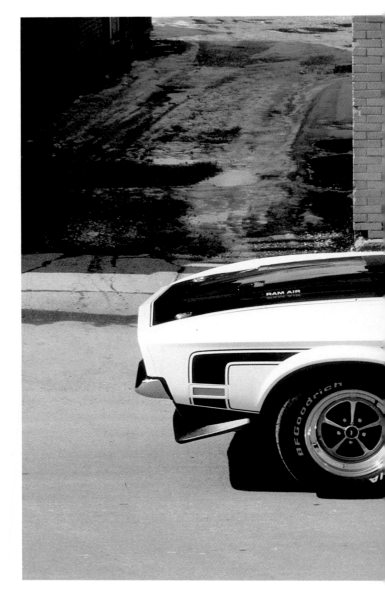

109 inches. With additional safety features like steel beam guards in the doors plus the extra sheet metal, weight also increased to the point where the '71 was 600 pounds heavier than the original 1964½ model.

The long-hood, short-deck theme continued unabated, though Ford had plenty of imitators. A long hood, short deck is attractive if proportions don't become over-balanced. This latest Mustang looked front-end heavy, suffering a little more than others of its type.

'71 STYLE

Up front, the grille cavity extended the width of the car. The grille itself was honeycombed hexagonal plastic set in an opening that stretched to the headlights. A horizontal bar cut across the middle of the grille from either side, meeting the traditional pony and corral in the center. Chrome trim extended from the leading edge of the front fenders across the hood lip to the opposite fender. Below the thicker bumper, the front valance was thinner, with parking and turn-signal lights at each end of the air slot.

The sides of the '71 were vast, flat expanses of steel broken only by raised molding running into the rear quarter panels. On some models the molding was covered by

*THESE PAGES. **A fine 1973 Mustang convertible – the last to be built for a decade.***

a plastic and chrome strip serving as a parking lot side-protector. Shinoda's GM lessons weren't forgotten, for the Mustang had the General's look inherent in its more pronounced "Coke bottle" design. Of the three body styles, the sportsroof wins as being the most dramatic, if not, dare one say, very practical. Its nearly horizontal roof extended all the way to the rear, earning itself the description of "flatback." It was almost impossible for the driver to use his rear-view mirror because he could hardly see anything. It was definitely the best mobile greenhouse yet devised, though.

At the rear the triple lens configurations were longer and clumsier than before, but the center lenses now contained the back-up lights. The rear panel was flat with the gas cap in the center as always. Looking at the rear of the fastback, one sees just a shade of Shelby's Daytona coupe. Whether this was intentional – and it is highly unlikely it was – the look is still certainly apparent.

The Boss 302 was gone, the semi-hemi Boss 429 was gone – the Grandé stayed, however. So did the Mach I, but it had changed – or its engine had. New was a Boss 351 sportsroof touted as a high-performance car. Total engine line-up consisted of the 250 cid six as standard, replacing the old 200, which was axed. Next came the 302 2V followed by five 351s in different variations from the standard 2V; a couple with Ram-Air and the Hi-Po unit as found in the Boss. Finally three 429CJs were offered.

Make no mistake. This 429 was a different animal from the semi-hemi monster and should not be confused

with it. It first appeared in 1970 powering Ford Torinos and Mercury Montegos. With the 428CJ gone, the 429 was the obvious choice for the Mach I.

Rated at 370 bhp gross, the 429CJ was built as a high-performance engine for the Mach I. Large valves, the largest yet used on a stock Mustang engine, hydraulic camming, strengthened rocker arms, high-lift camshaft, high-flow cylinder heads, and a 750 CFM Autolite were some of the many features of the 429CJ. There was also the 429SCJ – the Super Cobra Jet – with five extra horsepower, mechanical valve lifters instead of the hydraulic ones fitted to the CJ version, hotter cam, forged pistons, and a 780 CFM Holley carburetor. Strong and more durable, the 429SCJ was intended more for drag racing.

Roadtest magazine's test of the Mach I 429 SCJ-R (Ram Air) netted quarter mile runs of 14.433 to 14.815 seconds at 98.68 and 98.25 mph respectively. This was with a prototype which weighed more than the production versions, so those times were probably bettered, while the top speed was around 120 mph.

Much fleeter, faster, liked with reservation by the motoring media, the Boss 351 excelled over the 429CJ in most respects. "It produces a generous quantity of power for its size and yet is remarkably tractable and docile," reported *Car & Driver*. A high-lift cam was combined with short pushrods and wide stamped rocker arms, while stiffer valve springs were designed to withstand 5,400 rpm without float. The valve stems are chromed, and the engine featured domed aluminum pistons of great

strength, a cast-iron big port manifold which was attached to the big new 750 CFM Autolite 4 bbl carburetor. Lifters were mechanically operated. Many other features combined to make the 351 an engine to be reckoned with.

Its 0-to-60 times averaged 5.8 seconds and the quarter mile registered at about 14 seconds at 103 mph. Yet the car could yield 17 mpg on premium fuel if driven at normal road speeds. Its top speed was just a shade over 130 mph.

Unfortunately, its handling received less than enthusiastic reviews. *Car & Driver* had grave doubts about the suspension, comparing it to "short lengths of oak two by fours." And when the testers drove it on New York's worse-than-awful cratered streets, they complained the ride was like "some demented Chinese torture." As for cornering, that got the thumbs down, too, but the worst criticisms were kept for the view from the driver's seat. "It's like sitting in a bunker," they began. "You can hardly see out. The windows are gun slits, the belt line comes up almost to your chin and the horizontal rear deck and wide roof pillars block off all but a shallow field of vision directly to the rear." *Roadtest* echoed *Car & Driver's* views, stating lane changing was a potential hazard among the other things. *Road & Track*, too, in an owner survey, said that the Mustang had severe limitations because not enough money had been spent on the chassis and that it had a particularly deficient rear end. Sad to say, all these journals were right, but the inescapable fact was, to have these particular cars handle like an exotic

THIS PAGE. A rare one-year model indeed! Kansas dealers wanted something to bolster flagging 1970 sales, so the Twister was born. A Mach I with a slick paint job, only 96 Twisters were built, half with the mighty 428CJ V8, others made do with the 351 Cleveland.

and expensive European model, a buyer would have to pay as much as he would pay for a Ferrari. Enough said!

Both the Mach I and Boss 351 featured twin-function scoops drawing outside air into a sealed-air clean system. This was the Ram-Air option which could be ordered at no extra cost if the Mach I engine was the 302, yet the scoops were non-functional on the 351 or 429 unless Ram-Air was specified. A crazy situation.

A mini console was added as standard equipment to the completely revised interior: two huge round pods, one to the right with speedometer, the other to the left with a bunch of warning lights. A smaller central pod contained

the fuel gauge. The top of the dashboard was heavily padded and flat though the center section juts out toward the interior, serving as a home for radio and air conditioning units.

Returning for its third year was the Grandé luxury hardtop. A vinyl roof, as mentioned, was standard with a choice of four colors, while the interior was equipped with numerous luxury features optional in the other models. While base Mustangs and the Grandé featured chrome bumpers, both the Boss 351 and the Mach I had color-keyed urethane front bumpers as well as optional striping on the hood or body side.

ABOVE. *Grabbing for traction and burning rubber no doubt kept the tire makers happy. The culprit is a '73 Mach I with 351 power.*

ABOVE AND RIGHT. A 1973 Mustang convertible blends well with the fall colors; the interior is pure luxury.

LEFT. One of the nicer '72s, the one-year-only Sprint. This is the "Package B" version. Fewer than 800 Sprint hardtops were built, plus a mere 50 convertibles produced for Washington, D.C., and Virginia dealers. The car is readily identified by patriotic "U.S.A." shield on the rear fenders.

SALES FALL

Sales continued to drop all around in the pony-car market in particular and muscle cars in general. Mustang still remained number one with 149,678 units produced, compared to Camaro's 114,643. Poor little Barracuda had all but disappeared with only 18,678 being built. It was quite obvious the muscle-car/pony-car gloss was tarnishing rapidly. Iacocca's youth market had grown up, were raising families of their own, had new responsibilities to which super cars didn't fit. The auto companies, however, caught the drift quickly enough to offload their muscle cars before they began to strain them too much.

Like other car makers, Ford began dumping as well. First to go from the 1972 Mustang line-up was the 429, as well as the Boss 351. A limited production High Output 351, a modified version of the previous year's Boss, was offered early in 1972. In accordance with the increasingly stringent Federal emissions regulations, the engine's compression was lowered to 8.8:1 to enable it to use regular fuel. A camshaft with high valve lift for intake and exhaust was installed though the camming remained mechanical. Horsepower was now net, so at 266, it appeared to the uninitiated that the engine had lost 110 bhp, which of course it hadn't.

Three detuned 351s, the standard six, and the 302 were the only choices in a reduced line-up of cars that were virtually identical to the '71 models. To identify the year, the best place to look is the rear. In 1971 the word "Mustang" was in block letters across the deck-lid; in 1972 this became script lettering above the right taillight.

Most modifications related to items such as a new Exterior Decor Group, which included lower body side paint treatment, color-keyed front urethane bumper, and flat brushed aluminum hubcaps with trim rings.

The Mach I continued as Mustang's sole performance car, with a choice of either the 302 or one of the 351s to power it. On the luxury front, the Grandé continued

and offered a new two-tone accent stripe for the body sides. In February 1972 Ford introduced the Mustang Sprint. This was a cosmetic model offered in either Package A or Package B trim. All Sprints were white with dual blue stripes framed in red on the hood. On the dressy inside, the seats had white vinyl bolsters and blue cloth inserts. Other items with Package A included white-wall tires, while Package B offered all of Package A plus 15-inch Magnum 500 wheels.

Sales, however, crashed to Mustang's lowest point at 125,093 produced. This was almost double Camaro's 68,651, and Mustang could console itself with the fact that it was the only 1972 pony car to rack up six-figure sales. Cougar produced 52,702, while Firebird just pipped AMC Javelin's 27,176 at 29,951. Barracuda, as usual, was at the bottom of the list with only 16,142 built. In contrast, Chevrolet's four-cylinder subcompact Vega chalked up an impressive 394,592 sales compared to Ford's Pinto subcompact with 347,822 sold. It was 1960 all over again.

END OF THE FIRST GENERATION

"The Mustang market never left us; we left it." Lee Iacocca's remark about the situation had a strong ring of truth to it. He wanted to return to a smaller car, and by the time 1973 rolled around, the Mustang II was already scheduled for a 1974 launch. Therefore, 1973 was the final year for what is known as the "first generation" cars. What was to come wouldn't be remotely the same. Perhaps it's a good thing that the true Mustang departed when it did. It had passed its peak, and had it lingered on, it would have been compared to a fading star who is having just one more try, only to fail, to everyone's sorrow. It's best to go while you're still ahead. Mustang was beginning to get the appearance of having hung on too long, which is why it was better the curtain came down when it did.

Those last first-generation Mustangs were little changed from 1972. A new egg-crate grille, with vertical parking lights at each end, distinguished the '73 from the '72. The grille sat farther forward, with the centrally located pony now running in a deeper corral with chrome vertical bars at the top and bottom. A new chrome rectangular-shaped bezel framed the headlights while the bumpers were color-keyed urethane units designed to meet Federal 5-mile-per-hour impact requirements. The urethane was molded over a steel reinforcement bar, in addition to an impact beam and a pair of absorbers which, upon impact, pushed rearward and returned the bumper to its original position.

Five engine choices were offered again in 1973. The six, the 302, and three 351s, the latter being Mach I

options. These were either in "Cleveland" or "Windsor" form. Both engines had been introduced in 1969, though there were subtle differences between the two. For instance, the main bearing diameter in the Cleveland was 2.75 inches, in the Windsor 3.00 inches. Another oddity was the spark plug size. The Cleveland plugs fitted a 14-mm hole yet the Windsor's accepted an 18-mm circumference. While both engines had single two-barrel carburetors, the Cleveland was offered with a 4 bbl, but the Windsor was not.

Going down fighting, the Mach I still could be had with one performance engine, the 351 4V Cobra Jet. Rated at 248 bhp at 5,400 rpm, the CJ had several performance features including a cast nodular iron crankshaft, mechanical camshaft, high-load valve springs, and dual exhausts. Competition suspension and power front disk brakes were mandatory extra-cost options if this engine was ordered. A wide ratio four-speed manual or Cruise-O-Matic transmission was also extra cost because, curiously, there was no standard transmission. Talk about having your cake and eating it, too!

The Grandé continued as the luxury Mustang much as before comprising about 19 percent of 1973 production. This compares with 26 percent of Mach Is produced in the same year. A healthy 11 percent of all Mustang's 1973 sales were convertibles, as buyers rushed to get the last of this model type Ford intended to produce.

Here then lies a legend, the 1964½ Mustang, the pony nobody will every forget. An irreplaceable car born to give pleasure to millions. What had 1974 in store for Mustang's faithful?

OPPOSITE. *The pleasure of owning a Mustang – or any car for that matter – is to drive it. This one looks well driven by an owner who enjoys every mile he takes.*

BELOW. *The Plymouth Barracuda was nearest thing Chrysler had to a pony car until the 1970 Dodge Challenger. This is a '74 model, the last year it was made.*

BELOW RIGHT. *1972 Magnum 500 wheels were always a popular option.*

BOTTOM RIGHT. *The running horse motif featured on 1969 interior door panels.*

THESE PAGES. Midnight, Saturday.
Engines roar, cars quiver, the heat of
the exhausts blends with the warmth
of a summer's night... Ah! those were
the days. Cars ready to roll are: (left)
1969 Mach I 428, (center) 1970
Mach I 428 and (right) the awesome
1969 Boss 429.

5
A SHELBY IN NAME ONLY

A grand total of 3,225 Mustang-based Shelby GTs had sold in 1967. Of these, 1,175 were GT-350s while 2,050 had been GT-500s. It had been Shelby-American's best year to date. A sad aside was the demise of the legendary AC427 Cobra. The last was built in March 1967, two months after its second birthday. Total production of the 427 Cobra, including the few 428s built, was 348. Production of the 289 Cobra ended in 1965 after a run of 654 units spread over three years. When the final 427 drove out of the factory, there was nobody there to mourn its passing – apart from the Shelby-American employees, of course. No obituaries in the automotive press. Nothing. Only later did everybody realize what had disappeared from the scene.

Work on the 1968 Shelby GT-350 and GT-500 had begun during the summer of 1967. With the '67s selling so well, there was tremendous optimism in the Shelby camp that 1968 would be even better. If anything, the 1968 models would reflect public opinion digested from what customers voted for most on their option forms. It transpired they wanted the best of everything; snappy performance coupled with unashamed luxury, the leaning to luxury slightly more prevalent. Therefore the new GTs would have performance allied to boulevard pizzazz. Then the complications began.

Carroll Shelby had accomplished just about everything he had set out to do. His cars had raced all over the world with tremendous success; he had created a legend with the AC Cobra. His Ford connection was humming

along smoothly and successfully, so what more could a man want? His first instincts were for racing, but he had lost friends pursuing such a gamble. You either win or lose – or wind up dead. Anyway, his health excluded him from the track, so he set about trying to build a competitive racer in 1968. It was to be a car called the Cougar-Cobra for the Can-Am racing series, and it would be built in England.

One Cougar-Cobra was built. Then came trouble. Shelby had to change its name because Ford had acquired the Cobra nomenclature. So Shelby re-christened it the "Lone Star" instead. Next came a lack of sponsorship – Ford wasn't spending money like it once had – then the major problem was the car itself. Its rounded lines were attractive but dated. It was also underpowered. It was, to put it mildly, "DOA." Any racing Carroll Shelby had done in between trying to get the Lone Star off the ground was carried out in cars bought in from outside. The first was a Lola T-70, the next a McLaren M6. Peter Revson did the driving in both cars which were entered for the Can-Am series. The few events entered didn't exactly set the house on fire so Shelby finally decided to quit.

Two vexing problems arose regarding the production of the 1968 Shelby GTs. For one thing, supplies of high-quality fiberglass, essential for making certain sections of the car, were becoming increasingly difficult to obtain. Second, there was a problem with production space because North American wanted its hangars back. The

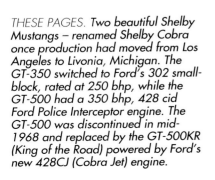

THESE PAGES. Two beautiful Shelby Mustangs – renamed Shelby Cobra once production had moved from Los Angeles to Livonia, Michigan. The GT-350 switched to Ford's 302 small-block, rated at 250 bhp, while the GT-500 had a 350 bhp, 428 cid Ford Police Interceptor engine. The GT-500 was discontinued in mid-1968 and replaced by the GT-500KR (King of the Road) powered by Ford's new 428CJ (Cobra Jet) engine.

LEFT. The poised Cobra motif adorning the front fenders ahead of the doors was new for '68. The pop-open gas cap (top above) also features the Cobra.

OPPOSITE. The Shelby GT500KR coupe – the KR stands for "King of the Road." Apart from the "KR" suffix, the car was identical to the stock GT500 it replaced; changes were all under the skin.

lease was about to expire with no chance to renew it, as the owners wanted the hangars for aircraft use. These problems were soon laid to rest. Henceforth, Shelby GTs would be produced by the A.O. Smith Company situated in Livonia, Michigan. This was a very advantageous arrangement for all concerned, particularly Ford. Livonia is just 10 miles north of Dearborn, and as Smith supplied Chevrolet with Corvette parts, the company had access to fiberglass. And as most of the responsibility for the Shelby GTs had been taken over by Ford, the move to Livonia was fortunate indeed.

SHELBY CONVERTIBLE

Once the dust had settled following the move, the A.O. Smith Company began producing the 1968 Shelby Cobra GTs (the Cobra name was used this year). The big news was the first Shelby convertible added to the line-up. This was available as either a GT-350 or GT-500 model. It had all the usual Shelby equipment including a

thickly padded roll-bar, the top of which was a shade flatter than the one used in the fastback.

Shelby's designers gave the '68 car a distinctive but attractive front end, thereby distancing it further from the standard Mustangs. Considering that the differences between the 1967 and 1968 models were almost inconsequential, the Shelby team had succeeded in giving their cars quite a distinctive look over the '67s.

Up front, a wider fiberglass nose jutted forward over the bumper and had a wide mesh grille set back deeply into the cavity. A pair of rectangular Lucas fog lights were set at each side of the mesh insert (some early Shelbys used Marchal fog lights, but problems forced them to be dropped). Below the bumper was a large opening cut out of the valance to permit better cooling, while the new fiberglass hood had large, functional twin air scoops at the extreme forward edge, a few inches behind the grille. Headlights were set in much the same fashion as the production Mustang. Thunderbird sequential taillights

ABOVE AND ABOVE RIGHT. Apart from the GT-350 or GT-500 emblem affixed to the instrument panel above the glove compartment, the different console with Stewart-Warner oil and amp gauges, a Cobra emblem on the center of the steering wheel, a standard, padded roll-bar, and the inertia seat belts, the interior of the Shelby is the same as that of the deluxe Mustang.

replaced those borrowed from the Cougar in 1967 and were mounted on the fiberglass satin-silver finished near panel which also housed the pop-open gas cap located in the center of the panel. The cap itself has the Shelby snake and the words "Shelby Cobra" embossed in the middle. Both the rear deck lid with its integral spoiler and quarter panel caps were fiberglass. In the center of the spoiler, the Shelby logos were spelled out in block letters and were repeated on the extreme front of the hood. Functional brake air-scoops decorated the rear quarter panels, and the roof air-vent scoop was also functional.

As for engines, the GT-350 got a new one for '68. This was the 302 four barrel rated at 250 bhp gross, and among its features was a Cobra aluminum intake and a 600 CFM Holley carburetor. Valve covers had the words, "Shelby – powered by Ford" emblazoned on the tops, while the oval air-cleaner had the inscription "Cobra."

Halfway through '68, the 428 cid V8 360 bhp Ford Police Interceptor engine, powering the Shelby Cobra GT-500 was replaced by the 428 Cobra Jet unit. The car

was suffixed GT-500KR, the KR standing for "King of the Road," the designation carried on the rocker panel stripe behind the front wheel opening.

Several changes made to the GT-500KR carried through to 1970. An extra brace consisting of quarter-inch-thick plate steel was wrapped around the lower edge of the shock tower, near the motor mounting. All cars ordered with four-speed manual transmissions had staggered rear shocks. Exclusive to the GT-500KR were wider rear brake shoes and drums. Heavy-duty brake line fittings, and heavy-duty wheel cylinders were also applied. As for horsepower, the 500KR was conservatively rated at 335, though it should really have been nearer 400.

On the inside, the Livonia-built Shelbys were all luxury, derived from the Deluxe Mustang Interior Group. A standard piece of equipment was the Shelby center console fitted with Stewart-Warner oil pressure and amperes gauges. An embossed Cobra insignia was carried on the padded armrest top, which also acted as a storage area. The snake also popped up in the center of the padded steering wheel spoke and on the door panels.

LEFT. The 500 KR interior was the same as the GT350/GT500.

BELOW. The 1968 GT350 sold half of the GT500's output, though it was probably more roadworthy. In deference to government regulations, all '68 Shelbys had side markers. 1965 T-Bird sequential lights replaced the previous year's Cougar unit.

The 1968 Shelby GT500KR
convertible is the most desirable of all
Shelbys for that year. The car had a
thick, padded roll-bar as standard.
Only 318 GT500KR convertibles
were ever built.

RIGHT AND FAR RIGHT. **The 1970 Shelby was the last of a fine breed; Ford bought the Cobra name and used it as a "go-faster" trim option on subsequent Mustangs beginning in 1976. Scoops abounded in 1970 – five on the hood alone – while the rear lights remain T-Bird sequentials.**

THE PRESS OPINION

"One thing about Carroll Shelby and his cars, they aren't subtle." So began the prestigious, sometimes infuriating, *Road & Track* magazine when it tested a Shelby GT-500. *Road & Track* tested Shelbys on several occasions over a five-year period. Whatever the editors liked about the look of them, the praise for the Shelby cars was soon dispelled when they got around to handling, steering and suspension. As far as these areas were concerned, the cars were unsophisticated and unsubtle.

Whatever *Road & Track* thought about the Shelbys' shortcomings, they, the editors, weren't alone. "The KR is at its best on a good road, smooth and fast," commented *Car Life*. "Nearly useless on anything but smooth surfaces," was the harsh judgment of *Car & Driver* which, in its inimitable style, went on to say the suspension on the 1969 Shelby GT-350 was so stiff that the car "bucks and weaves down a secondary road like a berserk go-kart."

Whichever way you look at it, America's automotive press was not overly impressed. Nothing about the Shelbys received harsher comment than the obviously none-too-pliant suspension.

The cure, however, was a question of price. Shelby didn't have the kind of money to make a silk purse out of a sow's ear. Ford had the money, but wouldn't spend it on what it considered an image car with limited potential. Shelby had to compromise.

No matter what the smart guys thought, everybody had to admit that Shelby had done wonders with the little he had to play with. The proof is with us today in this age of high-tech, super-sophisticated and, one has to admit, quite boring cars. Current collectors pay through the nose to get a Shelby GT Mustang. Forget the super-cools; if it's excitement or head-turning style you want or just plain character, go buy yourself a Shelby.

In 1968 Shelby GT-350s and GT-500s had their best sales year yet. Even with prices ranging from $4,116 to $4,594, total production was 4,450 with the GT-500s more popular by two to one. Ford entered 1969 with the Mach I and Boss 302, Shelby clones that would obviously compete head-on with the real thing. This competition did in fact have an adverse effect on the Shelbys.

As stated in the previous chapter, Mustang underwent a major restyle for 1969. Shelby-American stylists came

up with a new, cohesive, integrated design that worked well on the ever-growing pony car. For one thing it looked less like a production Mustang than ever before. Standard Mustangs, for instance, used four headlights; two in the grille and two in the flared front fenders. The redesigned Shelby used only two at each end of the wide, rectangular-shaped grille cavity. A wire mesh grille was inset into the opening and framed by a thin chrome rim. The Shelby snake and "Shelby" logo were attached to the driver's side of the grille. The cavity itself was trimmed, from the fender caps, across the hood, and down the other side by a wide chrome band which met the unique Shelby bumper to form a complete chrome frame not unlike – in fact, very similar to – the 1971 Mustang. Rectangular Lucas driving lights and parking lights are set under the bumper; the parking lights are at each end of the narrow valance opening.

The whole front end, including for the first time the front fenders, was fiberglass. Mustangs were getting heavier, hence the additional fiberglass pieces to help keep the weight down. The enormous fiberglass hood contained no less than five functional air-scoops. The three forward facing scoops were "V"-shaped, the centrally located one acting as air supplier to the Ram-Air air cleaner. The other two, positioned near the front of the hood, appear like entrances to tunnels due to the flattish, raised ridge molded into the hood on either side of the central scoop. These scoops feed air to the engine while the remaining two scoops, looking like tunnel exits, draw hot air away from it. It was scoops galore for 1969 Shelbys: each front fender contained vertical air-scoops ahead of the wheel openings to assist brake cooling. Scoops attached to the rear quarter panels also serve to duct air onto the rear brakes.

Like before, the rear deck lid and quarter panel extensions were fiberglass with a spoiler similar to the 1968 model. A black insert, edged in bright trim, ran the length of the spoiler with the word "Shelby" in block capitals contained within. A black rear panel sets off the 1965 Thunderbird sequential taillights carried over from 1968. Fat twin exhausts with rectangular openings jut out from the middle of the rear valance, while a hinged license-plate holder was mounted in the center of the rear panel and hid the fuel filler from view.

As can be seen from this 1977 model, the package looked reasonable; but when it came to performance, most Euro-boxes beat it with ease from the stoplight.

THESE PAGES. *The 1978 Cobra II was quite quick by American standards of the time. This fully optioned car is used daily and driven hard, which says something for its durability.*

THESE PAGES. *The mid-Seventies was a difficult period for U.S. auto makers contending with numerous Federal directives concerning safety and emissions. So there wasn't much Ford could do to give the Mustang II potency. Efforts to inject a little sparkle were tried in 1976 with the Cobra II. A Cobra in name only, it was essentially a dress-up kit, though the car was given a 302 V8 and handling suspension.*

INTERIOR LUXURY

Respecting people's needs, the Shelby's interior was more luxurious than ever. Like the 1968 models, it leaned heavily on Mustang's Deluxe Decor Group; lots of simulated wood panels dotted about and, of course, fake wood dashboard and glove compartment.

The center console had a Shelby-designed top section housing Stewart-Warner oil pressure and ammeter gauges, angled toward the driver. Two toggle switches, one for driving lights and the other for interior lights, were mounted in the rear section of the console. Round cobra emblems were attached to the wood grain applique door panel inserts. Fifteen- by seven-inch fine spoke wheels with cast aluminum centers and chrome rims were unique to Shelby GTs.

New for 1969 was the GT-350 engine. The 302 departed after only one year to be replaced by a 351 4V Windsor and rated at 290 bhp. Shelby modifications included an aluminum high-rise intake manifold and hydraulic lifter cam. Finned aluminum valve covers state "Cobra – Powered by Ford." A 470 CFM Autolite four barrel sat astride the manifold. A four-speed manual transmission was standard with automatic as optional. Among the options were a Traction-Loc rear end and 3.00 to 3.50 axle ratios.

The insignia "428 Cobra Jet" on the die-cast valve covers distinguished the GT-500. Conservatively rated at 335 bhp gross, the 428 CJ was given a 735 cfm Holley 4 bbl carburetor which was on the aluminum medium-rise intake manifold. A high-capacity fuel pump completed the picture. The same Ford top loader four-speed transmission was standard with a 3.50 rear end. Other options were the same as the GT-350.

Shelby-American entered a pair of 302-powered cars in the 1969 Trans-Am racing series. Driven by Peter Revson and Horst Kwect, the Shelbys proved tremendously fast, but the only factory-prepared car to win one out of 12 events was driven by Sam Posey. Then, on August 3, 1969, at the St. Jovite track, Shelby's two cars featured in a hefty pile-up on the track. Injuries were minor, but Shelby's cars, plus a Bud Moore that had also been entered by Shelby, were totaled. Photographs of the accident showed the cars in a hideous mess.

SHELBY RETIRES

On October 4, 1969, Carroll Shelby officially announced his retirement from racing. He hung up his famous black cowboy hat for the last time. He had been becoming disenchanted for some time.

In 1969, 1279 GT-350s and 1871 GT-500s, totaling 3,150 units in all, had been sold. This was a drop of 1,300 over 1968, but could be attributed to buyers steering clear of sports and muscle cars in general. It was an industry-wide problem with no immediate answer in sight. As for Shelby, his involvement with Ford had come to an end. At one time his Mustang-based GTs filled an empty slot in the pony-car line-up, serving to promote performance. Now Ford had brought in its own home-built muscle in the shape of the Mach I, Boss 302, and Boss 429, and was spending an increasing amount of time at the

tracks itself. Shelby's contribution had become redundant.

All this was a shame. Shelby represented, whatever the critics might say, a pinnacle of the American motor performance art. It was he, after all, who helped engineer Ford past the winning post at Le Mans. Holman and Moody were there too, that great June day in 1966, their mechanical knowhow invaluable to the cause.

Europeans had sneered. Such lack of sophistication, they said arrogantly. Well, they had to eat their words when Detroit's unsophisticates showed Europe's overengineered prima donnas the way to the door. It had always been Shelby's dream to make Ferrari and the rest eat dirt. He did it, not only at Le Mans, but at other events, in other championships, with his classic Cobras. The United States owes a debt to Shelby because it was he, virtually alone, who taught the Europeans a lesson, who beat them at their own game and earned their respect in the field of motoring competition.

Although Shelby announced the end of his involvement with Ford in 1969, 1970 was actually the final year for the Shelby GTs. In fact, the 1970 models were 1969 cars given a minor visual update. Two black stripes appeared on the hood and a black plastic spoiler identical to those used on the '69 Boss 302s was added to the front lower valance. Modifications were carried out at Ford's Kar Kraft facility famous for building GT-40s in 1966 and 1967. A grand total of 315 GT-350s and 286 GT-500s was produced, 601 in all. Some of these cars were actually dressed-up Mach Is. They are easy to spot because they may have had red or tan interiors and other items not listed on Shelby's order sheet.

Ford, however, had bought the Cobra name and took full advantage of it. First were the Cobra Jet engines, great powerhouses all. Then, in an effort to give the little Mustang II some sparkle, Ford offered the Cobra II in 1976. This was essentially a dress-up kit option available only on the three-door hatchback body. It came in white with twin black hood stripes and a black rocker panel stripe carrying the "Cobra II" insignia emblazoned across the length of the door.

A sports steering wheel, dual remote outside mirrors, brushed aluminum appliqués on the dash panel and door inserts, blacked-out grille, flip-open quarter windows covered with plastic louvers, and the inevitable simulated hood scoop were other features in a long list of go-faster bits. Also included were stylish steel wheels, front and rear spoilers, and Cobra decals on the front fenders. The Cobra on the grille was plastic, which sums up the car.

Under the hood was an emissions-strangled 302 single barrel V8. In its then rather anemic form, it couldn't pull the skin off a rice pudding. Rated at 139 bhp net, there was no doubt this engine had potential, though buried under a fuel crisis, Federal harassment, and general frustration, nobody had discovered it yet.

ABOVE. Cobra II's final curtain call was in 1978. Separated from the memory of its buccaneering ancestors, the Cobra II wasn't all that bad.

Snakes, numbers, letters, stripes, they were everywhere in what must be regarded as the ultimate in "go-faster" dress. Actually quite a collectible car, this rare 1978 King Cobra is loaded with every option. It appeared for one year only and could do the quarter-mile in 17 seconds.

KING COBRA

Different color schemes were offered for the 1977 Cobra II, but the car remained the same as in 1976. In 1978 Ford tried to interest all and sundry with an even more flamboyant go-faster, paint-on performance package. This was the King Cobra. Taking a leaf out of Pontiac's Trans-Am book – the eagle splattered across the hood – Ford shoved a gold decal on the Mustang's hood which, to all the world, probably looked like a Cobra which had met with an unfortunate accident crossing the road one night! Anyway, there it was, now flattened on the King Cobra's hood.

Tape stripes on the roof, T-tops, more stripes on the rear deck and rocker panels, a black "basket handle" wrapping over the rear roof section, a massive front spoiler – air dam if you will – extending back to the flared front wheel arches. The words "King Cobra" decorated the doors and rear deck spoiler. Grille, window moldings, windshield wipers, and headlight bezels had a matte black finish: Ford PR said it was sporty – which was

one way to say it's cheaper than chrome!

As with other Cobras, the King was equipped with a 302 cid V8, power steering, and "Rally" handling package. To be fair to these kiddy Cobras, they weren't all that bad. To be able to turn in a quarter-mile run in 17 seconds was fairly cantering back in '78! Due to their diminutive size, they were quite nippy in traffic and not at all uncomfortable.

Cobra dress-up kits continued into the third-generation Mustangs launched in 1979. The squashed-cobra look remained splayed across the hood much to the annoyance of the automotive press. Michelin TRX radial tires combined with TRX special suspension were much more to the point, and the cars were at last beginning to perform and handle with reasonable alacrity. And, harking back to the Sixties, there was a choice of two engines; the 302 V8 or an overhead cam four-cylinder unit, which was turbo-charged, no less.

The cars were beautifully styled in the European mode. Detroit thought it was classy to look European, though the

*THESE PAGES. **The third-generation Mustang arrived in 1979 with another Cobra dress-up kit. It could be had with a 302 V8 or a turbo-charged four-cylinder 140 cid. 115 mph and 0-60 in 9 seconds was fair for the V8 models, but the turbo-four was a disappointment with its 105 mph top and 11.5 to 12 seconds to reach 60.***

author is of the opinion that this is nonsense, and that current European and Japanese designs represent one almighty yawn. Class is art, not ergonomics.

Road testers, however, found the third-generation cars handled reasonably well even if rutted roads still threw them a bit. As for acceleration, the cars were beginning to move once again. The 302, for instance, could crack standstill to 60 in 9 seconds, while the turbo-charged four managed 11.5, which was a little disappointing.

Another somewhat watered-down "Cobra" appeared in 1981. The 255 cid (4.2 liters) V8 was the largest engine available, and the ornate hood Cobra detail and side stripes were there for the asking.

That appeared to be the end. As the Eighties wore on, true performance could be had with the GT models and the sparkling SVO, so there was no need for a Cobra to provide muscle. A dozen years were to go by when Ford decided to take out the 14-year-old design with a bang. A Special Vehicles Team Group was formed with the express purpose to create lively, high-tech sporty cars.

In January 1993, the results of SVT's endeavors was announced: the 1993½ Mustang Cobra 5.0L coupe. Only 5,000 were to be built of the special high-performance car, primarily to keep enthusiast interest on the boil, and to have something to fire a broadside at the new Pontiac Firebird and Chevrolet Camaro models.

Pushing out 235 hp, or 30 more than the standard GT, the Cobra was quickly snapped up by Mustang devotees. 4,993 were actually built, and the model received the dubious distinction as being one of the hottest cars to steal. On the plus side, the Cobra handled well, bearing in mind the limitations of a live rear axle. Steering was very precise, cornering abilities excellent, but dumping all that power on a slightly wet pavement would produce results akin to a maddened alligator.

More Cobra models are destined with Mustang's swish new design. They promise to be very high tech and far better than anything that has gone before. Still, there's nothing to replace the days of the Sixties when rough, tough real Shelbys were truly "Kings of the Road."

*THESE PAGES. **The 1993½ Cobra was launched to keep interest alive in the old body and the car had plenty of muscle like its breatheren of 25 years before.***

143

6
THE END OF AN ERA
AND A NEW BEGINNING

Lee Iacocca wanted to get back to basics. He openly disapproved of the way his brainchild was developing. After Bunkie Knudsen, the Mustang was getting bigger and fatter, with the result that it was losing sight of its original concept. The pony-car/muscle-car boom had gotten out of hand, had been overdone. Consequently, the public had tired of them, had stayed away from them, and so sales were beginning to slip.

There's little doubt Iacocca saw the writing on the wall long before anyone else. The presidency of Ford was still a little more than a year away when Iacocca flew to Italy late in 1969 accompanied by his close friend, Hal Sperlich, one of the Mustang's original team. They went to Ghia's studios and told Alejandro de Tomaso what they wanted. As we have already seen, Ghia's prototype for the Mustang II arrived a couple of months later. There was no argument: this was to be the basis for the new car.

No inspired guesses, no playing hunches this time. Iacocca had been watching the rising sales of the European and Japanese imports, particularly their sporty "personal" cars. It must have been galling to observe an American idea returning to Uncle Sam as a foreigner. Some, like Ford's Capri, a more or less direct copy of the original Mustang, were captive imports. Toyota wasn't, but displayed no hesitation in lifting Mustang's taillight

design almost intact and sticking it on the back of the Celica. As Iacocca watched import sales go up and up, he knew this time it was no gamble. The folks out there wanted a small car.

It was nearly a repeat performance of the original Mustang's birth. Stylists and engineers met and talked and compared ideas; Iacocca told them the new Mustang had to have a wheelbase of 96 to 100 inches and a four-cylinder engine as standard, with a six as an optional. It had to be strong on quality, have plush but sporty interiors, and come as a fastback and hardtop coupe. Ford's styling studios went to work; so did Lincoln-Mercury's studios – after all, they knew something about sporty cars because they had the Cougar and the Anglo-German Capri which was sold through L-M dealers.

Five clay models, a hardtop coupe, and four fastbacks were submitted for approval. After much deliberation, Lincoln-Mercury's fastback design was chosen to act as basis for the eventual Mustang II. Actually, the design was a hodgepodge of ideas taken from Ghia, Ford, and L-M stylists. Once everything had been thrown together, the clay became a cohesive whole. Target date was fall 1973 for launching the second-generation Mustang as a '74 model. Lee Iacocca couldn't have planned it better if he'd tried.

ABOVE AND LEFT. European flavor was provided by Italian coachbuilding firm, Ghia, with an American blend. Mustang Ghia was a luxury model with a soft ride four-cylinder or V6 power. The 1976 model shows sunroof and Euro-style amber turn signal lights.

FAR LEFT. 1974 saw the birth of Mustang II. Standard engine was 140 cid, 85 bhp in-line four, the complete opposite of what went before.

ABOVE. *The 1975 Mustang Mach I was a far cry from the first-generation model; the standard engine was a 171-cubic-inch V6. A 302 cid V8 was an option, though.*

THE IMPACT OF CRISIS

October 1973: the West was reeling in a state of shock at the Middle East oil crisis. It never works to become as complacent as the industrialized world had over the ready availability of oil. Suddenly it was in short supply, bringing home the stark realization of how reliant society had become on the black stuff.

If the stock markets, governments and finance houses had been badly jolted – and they were – what about Detroit? Oil is an automobile's lifeline. It feeds it, succors it, lubricates its multitude of moving parts. The sudden oil price escalation coupled with a shortage was a painful kick below the belt. The motoring giants had no contingency plans for a crisis such as this. Panic reigned in the boardrooms. Apart from a few compacts, none of the cars then in production had any claim to economical running. The vehicles Detroit had on their back lots were big, thirsty cars. Then to cap it all, the Federal government brought into law the 55 mph national speed limit.

Panic had also begun down at street level. Gas lines formed, tempers blew up as gas pumps ran out. One California man was shot to death at a filling station. Fortunately, the public has a greater degree of adaptability than big corporations. The big Detroiters were shunned in favor of economical little European and Japanese – especially Japanese – cars. One company, Ford, had at least one car with which to compete against the invading hordes. Courtesy of Lee Iacocca, for whom the oil crisis had arrived as if planned, Ford had the Mustang II.

It met with guarded reviews from the automotive press. "Humpy and bumpy," sniffed *Road & Track*. *Consumer Guide Auto Test '74* liked its interior, but concluded that "Ford could have done a still better job," and that "the Mustang is no match for the Capri." Certainly nobody was overstruck by its styling, least of all Mustang's faithful followers, who felt cheated and let down. All in all it was not an overly enthusiastic reception for a new car. In better times, the lukewarm reviews would have killed it. But it wasn't better times and that, in a nutshell, is probably what saved it and sold it.

Two models, a hardtop coupe and fastback offered in seven series, from the standard two-door to the Mach I three-door hatchback – fastback, call it what you will – arrived in the showrooms during that grim fall of '73. To keep its price down (a standard two-door coupe cost $3,134 in 1974), Ford engineers followed much the same procedure as they had with the original Mustang. They cannibalized chassis, engine, and suspension from the little Pinto's spare's bin.

PINTO AND THE MUSTANG

Because of this component sharing, many initially condemned the Mustang II as a souped-up Pinto. They shared the same 140 cubic-inch (2.3 liter) inline four-cylinder engine: although built in the U.S., it had originated from Ford Europe, which had designed it for Cortinas and for British and German Capris.

In the Mustang II's case, this engine was standard, but optional on the Pinto, which used a smaller engine as its base power plant. Also shared was the front suspension consisting of unequal length upper and lower arms. One immediate difference between the two was Mustang's lower arm. This was attached to a rubber-mounted subframe while the Pinto arm was bolted to the body structure. Both cars employed leaf springs at the rear but the Mustang's were two inches longer and used staggered shocks.

Differences manifested themselves in other areas, too. Although both cars were of unit-body construction, Mustang's subframe assembly and its design had the advantage of a better, smoother ride by isolating the rear engine mount from the body structure, thereby preventing annoying drive-train vibration from getting through to the passengers. The Pinto, an altogether cheaper car, lacked these refinements.

While both used rack and pinion steering, the Mustang's was further refined by mounting it differently to minimize shock. In fact, the Mustang's steering was one area approved by road-testers because it was light and precise. Standard steering was manual with 4.1 turns lock-to-lock, while the optional power steering was quicker at 3.3 turns. It was the opinion of many that the manual was probably superior due to its precise control and degree of road feel.

When it came to bodywork, the Pinto and Mustang II went their separate ways. There was a similarity, but it was probably due more to corporate identity than anything else. Interestingly, some features found on the Pinto were actually designed for the Mustang II; hence the Pinto upgraded itself on the back of its sportier cousin.

*BELOW. **A fully dressed 1978 Mustang II hatchback with T-tops.***

MUSTANG II, A BEAUTIFUL CAR?

By no stretch of the imagination could the Mustang II be called beautiful. In no way, whichever way you look at it, could it be considered a classic. The stylists tried to recreate some of the old Mustang magic by using similar sculpturing along the sides, which ended, remember, with the first of many simulated scoops. At least the Mustang II didn't get a scoop, fake or otherwise.

The grille and entire front end bore a distinct resemblance to the 1964½–1967 Mustang, although they were smaller and made of plastic! The grille was a cross-hatch affair with rectangular parking lights set at either end. In the center was the traditional pony, now galloping wild and free because he'd lost his corral. Headlights were set into plastic chrome square bezels above the color-keyed urethane 5 mph safety bumper, which contained a thin, black rubber molding edged in white trim. Even the bumper tried, albeit very crudely, to emulate the shape of its illustrious forebear.

In profile the coupe version displayed a truncated long–hood, short–deck theme which didn't sit very well. As *Road & Track* said, it looked humpy and dumpy with too high a waistline which dipped in the center, creating a rather odd effect, especially viewed from three-quarters front. There was a tendency to round off the curves, which is all very well if the line follows through to the

roof. Perhaps this is where all those different designs thrown together didn't help, for the notchback roof was a formal, rather square design that didn't match the lower half at all satisfactorily. If that was not enough, the wheels looked far too small for the rest of the car.

The hatchback model was a much better design altogether. There was still a pudginess about it, but the roofline blended well with the rest of the body, flowing in a continuous sweep to the rear panel. This housed triple taillights on either side, though they were much larger and more ornate than the original designs on the earlier models. The large hatchback lid lifted up and was held in position by self-supporting telescopic struts. Trunk room on the coupe was a bit sparse, having only 10 cubic feet of space. By folding down the hatchback's rear seat, an enormous 28 cubic feet of room could be added to the trunk space.

Disk brakes were standard at the front with drums at the rear. Wheel size was 13 inches clad in standard BR70X 13 tires. Radial tires were standard on all models, helping the car's roadability immeasurably. Two transmissions were available. The standard unit, which was also standard on the Pinto, was a four-speed manual based on the British gearbox, strengthened to cope with the Mustang's extra power. Ford's three-speed automatic was the other option.

A German Ford-built, 171 cubic-inch (2.8 liter – measurements were metric, so cubic inches were replaced by liters), single overhead cam V6, rated at 105 bhp (the four was 85 bhp) was an option in all save the Mach 1 where it was standard. Powering the Mach 1, a rather sad excuse for what went before, the V6 propelled the car from 0-60 in 13-9 seconds which, considering the engine, wasn't all that bad. Top speed was a little over 100 mph, again quite respectable when all the power-sapping emissions controls are taken into account. By way of contrast, four-cylinder Mustangs could reach 60 from standstill in around 17 seconds.

QUALITY IMPROVES

One area much improved through Iacocca's insistence was quality control and upgraded interior fittings. If nothing else, Mustang IIs were very well put together, panels fitted and matched well, and the paint looked good. Interior trim and fixtures reached a very high standard, with a choice of pleated cloth or vinyl upholstery. Top-grade leather was a desirable option. Whatever the choice, road-testers found seat comfort to their liking, some even claiming it was actually better than Mustangs of old. In the back was a rear seat of little use to anyone but small children or anybody the car's owner didn't like.

Instrumentation was surprisingly good for a car of this type, and it served to accentuate the glamorous interior. The dashboard was a heavily padded cowl covering the instrument panel. Two large round dials housed a tachometer and speedometer, with three rather small dials clustered in line to the right. These served as fuel, temperature, and oil gauges. They were perhaps a shade too small because quite a number of people complained they were hard to read. Standard heating or optional air conditioning controls and radio were mounted on the left and right of the steering column. The steering wheel itself was quite large, with a single, padded, boomerang-shaped spoke. The shift column, manual or automatic, was mounted on the fairly high, central transmission hump.

Fake wood on the instrument panel plus a vinyl-wrapped steering wheel was part of the luxury Ghia interior option, standard on the Ghia coupe, but extra on other models. European-type armrests, thicker carpeting, two-tone soft vinyl upholstery and grab handles made up the package, which added only $96 to a base Mustang.

Fitting for the type of model, the Mach I came with the optional handling package. This included adjustable shock absorbers, anti-roll bars front and rear, as well as staggered (adjustable) rear shocks and stiffer springs. In this guise the Mustang II, no matter whether it was a Mach I or standard hardtop, handled quite well. Not so the Ghia, complete with its vinyl roof, luxury interior, and Ghia badges on the rear roof pillars. Its suspension was as squelchy as a cream puff. It is extraordinary how a car's character can be completely changed by altering a few suspension settings.

Overall length of the Mustang II was 175 inches sitting on a 96.2-inch wheelbase. The height was 49.6 inches and width 70.2 inches. Fuel economy averaged 23.5 mpg with the four-cylinder engine, around 19-20 if the six was specified. One of the penalties of using the V6 was the car's disproportionate front/rear weight imbalance: 57 percent over the front, only 43 percent at the rear. It made the Mach I equipped with the handling package look like a fairly decent little car.

THESE PAGES. The '78 Mustang II hatchback in detail. The brushed aluminum appliqué instrument panel, 302 cid V8, wire wheels, and garish two-tone body colors are more suited to a mid-Fifties car, but they provided a striking combination nevertheless in Mustang II's final year.

The all new third-generation Mustang was launched for 1979. As had happened on previous designs, several FoMoCo styling teams competed with each other, and the eventual winner was a team headed by Jack Telnack, executive director of Ford North American Light Truck & Car Design. The car shown is a hatchback with turbocharged version of the four-cylinder engine.

The 1979 Mustang Ghia hardtop
shows heavy European influence,
especially in the Mercedes-like rear
window and C-pillar.

THESE PAGES. Mustang was chosen to pace the 1979 Indy 500, and to celebrate, Ford produced a limited edition replica of the Pace Car. It had special cloth upholstery, unique side decals, and "MUSTANG" in large orange letters on each side of the hood scoop. The engine was the perennial 302 V8.

NOT FOR PURISTS

The true Mustang purists hated the Mustang II, and to this day few people will recognize it. It is said that the Mustang Club of America took sympathy and have given it recognition. Other clubs and localized affiliates, however, still refuse to give it a chance. Most Mustang books and magazines only concentrate on the 1964½ to 1973 models. It might be worth saving a few, though they have a horrid weakness to rust.

Once again, however, Lee Iacocca had been proved right. Though few of the cars sold to Mustang diehards, 385,993 Mustang IIs were produced, just 10 percent fewer than the 12-month total production for the first Mustang. That record 12-month production was eclipsed only by Ford's compact Maverick, which had a first-year sales record of 450,000 units.

As people got used to paying more for gas now that oil was on tap again (it wasn't off for long, anyway), interest waned a little in smaller cars. But with Corporate Average Fuel Economy (CAFE) instigated by an administration determined that citizens should conserve oil rather than guzzle it like before, Detroit was tooling up for a program of smaller, more down-sized cars; making all of them more fuel efficient. If they didn't, the Government would penalize them severely to the tune of millions of dollars. So smaller cars it would have to be.

From 1974 to 1978 the Mustang II changed very little, if at all. The 302 V8 was offered as an option in 1975 and developed 122 bhp net. This was increased to 139 bhp for 1976 to 1978. In 1975 a flip-up glass "moonroof" was a new option offered at $454. T-tops came in during 1978 as part of a Mach I option. It came with brushed aluminum dash panel, a three-spoke vinyl-covered sports steering wheel, a black vinyl "basket han-

dle" – also offered on the Mach I – as well as thick carpeting and luxuriant upholstery.

By 1978 the price of the base model had jumped $600. Much of this increase could be attributed to additional emissions controls such as the catalytic converter. As far as sales were concerned, the Mustang II never again reached its first-year production totals. Sales dipped to their lowest point in 1977 when 153,173 were produced, but it bounced back to almost half of the 1974 figure in 1978, its final year.

END OF THE MUSTANG II

Nobody really mourned the Mustang II's passing. The enthusiasts certainly didn't. Go-faster stripes, cobras on the hood, Italian design features, none of these extras could halt the car's middle-aged spread. No longer were the young buying Mustangs; it had become the choice of elderly ladies, schoolteachers, nice people who wanted to be just a little daring without really being noticed.

At the halfway point – 1976 to be exact – Ford decided a totally new Mustang was needed. It would be launched as a 1979 model, yet its design would be stylish enough to carry it into the mid-Eighties and beyond. This would be Mustang's third-generation model and as different from the other two as chalk is from cheese. Furthermore, it would have to recapture the excitement of the first-generation Mustang: its youth, its style, its freedom of expression, like the pony it was meant to represent.

Once again, the final design was selected from several submitted by various Ford Motor Company styling teams. The winning entry blended the best from the other studios in its design, which was the work of a team led by Jack Telnack. He was executive director of Ford's North American Light Truck and Car Design, which

played a major role in the styling of the Ford Fiesta.

A lot of work went into the new Mustang's final shape. Aerodynamics were beginning to play an increasing role in automotive design, once it was realized a low drag factor enhanced fuel economy. Ford was at the forefront of this school of thought, with its designers placing great reliance on wind tunnel testing.

The third-generation Mustang was one car to be influenced by wind-tunnel testing (a total of 136 hours in all). Not long after came the Probe design exercises leading to Ford's current aerodynamic shapes which are without doubt the best-looking, most individual crop of cars available anywhere in the world.

As with previous Mustangs, the new one had its host-model. This time it was the soon-to-be-announced Ford Fairmont/Mercury Zephyr compacts. It had a different body, of course, but it would be built on the new compact floorpan somewhat modified to take Mustang's 5.1-inch shorter wheelbase. Base suspension was hived off from the Fairmont/Zephyr cars, as were the MacPherson struts at the front with coil springs and its shock absorbers and anti-roll bar. A four-bar link rear suspension, coils and shocks took care of the solid axle. Whatever happened to independent suspension, once promised on a few competition Mustangs more than 12 years earlier? A rear anti-roll bar was compulsory on models provided with a V8.

Talking about V8s, the new Mustang's engine choices were the same as for the Mustang II; a 140 cid, 88 bhp SOHC four; 171 cid, 109 bhp V6 and a V8 of 302 cubic inches and rated at 140 bhp. The four-cylinder engine was standard fare, but an interesting variation of the four was the turbocharged version.

TURBO-POWER

It was the first time Mustang had offered turbocharging on any of its models. It was quite a clever idea: a turbine positioned in the exhaust gases flow is connected to an impeller close to the carburetor. Nothing much happens during normal driving because the impeller turns too slowly. Pushing the accelerator pedal to the floor speeds up the engine, which in turn increases the exhaust gas flow. As the flow increases, so too does the turbine, followed by the impeller. Now things begin to happen deep within the engine bay. As the impeller's speed increases, the pressure of the air-fuel mixture fed to the combustion chambers also increases. Net result: more power.

THESE PAGES. *A 1983 Mustang convertible at speed. The third-generation model improved as each year passed, though an otherwise attractive interior is marred by tacky wood appliqué treatment.*

Equipped with the turbo option, the 2-3 liter four could do 0-60 in about 11.5 seconds, which wasn't bad considering the stifling emissions controls and the 2,776 pounds of curb weight. Then again, it wasn't good enough compared to European cars like VW's Scirocco which could take on, and beat, the blown Mustang with a non-turbocharged engine while delivering 10 mpg better mileage figures. Owners and testers were none too impressed with the turbo Mustang in its infancy. They cited its unreliability among other things, such as a very definite lag in the response time between the accelerator and the turbo.

Three transmissions – four-speed manual, four-speed manual with overdrive (V6 and V8 only), and three-speed automatic – were available. Later in 1979, Mustang took delivery of a 200 cid in-line six rated at 85 bhp net. Why a straight-line six when Mustang already had a V6? Quite simply, supplies of the German-made engine ran short, hence the substitution.

It's worth mentioning the suspension again, because it was quite a change from previous designs. As we saw earlier, the new Mustang was given McPherson struts at the front in place of upper A arms, and the old "carthorse" leaf spring arrangement was done away with in favor of coils. Ford's engineers settled on three systems

for the 1979 car: standard, as described; "handling" and "special." The latter was the most interesting, transforming mediocre handling, with all the horrors it entails, into a near-perfect combination of good ride and controllable behavior, bearing in mind the inherent limitations of the car's suspension set-up.

That the suspension was pliant is due partly to the Michelin low-profile TRX radial tires. These had already been used to good effect on the European Ford Granada. Tire size was 65R 390 and were mounted on forged aluminum wheels, part of the "special" suspension package. The suspension itself had its own shock absorber valving, high near-spring rates, and thicker front and rear stabilizer bars.

The middle-of-the-road handling suspension was available only with 14-inch radials and featured stiffer springs, shocks, and front stabilizer bar – as mentioned before, a rear stabilizer was compulsory if the V8 was ordered.

Rack and pinion steering was carried over from the Mustang II with power assist as an option. Many magazine testers liked the precise feel of the steering and considered it unnecessary to go for the power-assisted variable ratio system. If going for the V8 engine, it was probably wiser to specify power assist though. And most customers did just that.

Another option, albeit ringing suspiciously of gimmickry, was a "vehicle systems monitor." This was a graphic display unit set in the console which showed a car's silhouette. Warning lights were placed in strategic places on the silhouette to tell the driver of low fuel, low windshield washer fluid, and inoperative headlights, taillights and brake lights. There was also a quartz digital chronometer which displayed time, date, and elapsed time at the press of a button.

Certainly the body of the 1979 Mustang owed much to European design. So much so that on first acquaintance one could be forgiven for mistaking it for a German car. The shape was angular, racy almost, with its laid-back black plastic crosshatch grille flanked by dual rectangular headlights. The rear roof pillars were wide, particularly on the hatchback, and had black slats behind the quarter windows, a styling ploy reminiscent of the Mercedes 450 SLC.

Of the two designs, notchback and hatchback, the most attractive was the latter, especially in its rear quarter panel treatment. There was quite a slope to the design at the front, no doubt the result of wind tunnel tests, which produced a drag coefficient of 0-44 for the fastback, 0-46 for the notchback.

To help save weight, a lot of plastics, aluminum and thinner metal and glass were used. The bumpers had reaction-injection-molded soft urethane covers emphasized

by a raised, matte black rubbery plastic band that encircled the lower half of the car from end to end, rather in the fashion of a fairground bumper car for want of a better description. Use of weight-saving steels, plastics and alloys, all of higher strength due to high-tech methods of manufacture, Ford's engineers saved some 200 pounds over the Mustang II, which was smaller by four inches.

'79 MODELS

The 1979 Mustang came in only hatchback and notchback forms, but as four models: base two-door, base three-door, and Ghia two-door and three-door. The Ghia model was the dressed-up version. Then there was the Cobra kit, available with turbocharged Mustangs; the flattened snake refused to leave the hood it seems. And the pony – where was the traditional pony? It appears that when it was let out of its corral on the Mustang II, it took off, never to be seen again. In its place was just the inscription "Ford" in small block letters on the left-hand side of the grille.

Despite the beginnings of a sales downturn that was soon to reach epidemic proportions in the early 1980s, the new Mustang sailed through 1979 with a healthy 332,025 units produced. The recession really began to make itself felt by 1981, and it is said that Ford was in poor shape, surviving on the back of its profitable British and German outlets. (Ford has been number one in sales in the British Isles for as long as anyone can remember.)

Today, however, Ford is in a sound financial position through its excellent designs and superior quality of all its products, from Fiesta to Continental, and is snapping at GM's heels more lustily than ever before. Nobody thought much of Ford's worries in 1979, which was all to the good. Most people's attention instead was taken up with Chrysler, whose future looked scant indeed. But Chrysler, America's third largest automobile company, was pulled back from the brink by the incomparable Lee Iacocca, who had performed his magic once again.

INFLUENCE OF EUROPE

There was a great deal of European influence in the new Mustang's styling, even down to its interior controls situated on two stalks, one on each side of the steering column. The left stalk operated turn signals, headlight dimmer, and horn, while the one on the right controlled the windshield wiper/washer combination.

If the car was ordered with tilt steering, a third, smaller stalk was added to control its movements. Intermittent wipers, rear defogger, cruise control, and air conditioning were part of the huge list of options, though safety-ori-

ented items such as rear defogger and intermittent wipers were standard by necessity. Even now, most cars coming from Detroit still list the above as options, which is nothing short of disgrace. Items like this should be mandatory on all cars, as should anti-lock brakes, which have at least been made standard on recent higher-priced cars, though only optional on others. It's a move in the right direction and the car makers are to be praised for it. So come on Detroit, at least make rear window defoggers standard!

IACOCCA FIRED!

Iacocca, as we all know, had put Ford back on the map with the Mustang. His loyalty to Ford reached farther back than his 32 years with the company: it went back to the days when his father drove Fords, back to that time when he first saw a 1940 Lincoln Continental at close hand. That had been the day he decided Ford was where he wanted to be. But, on July 13, 1978, a month after the press previews for the 1979 Mustang, Lee Iacocca was summoned by Henry Ford II. Shortly afterward, he left, dumbfounded, hurt beyond comprehension, not quite believing what had happened. He had just been fired.

It is not the purpose of this book to explore the decisions of Henry Ford II. Much has already been written about Ford's decision to fire perhaps the best man ever to work for him. For the full story, read Iacocca's graphic account in his book *Iacocca: An Autobiog-raphy*. A viewpoint expounded in Iacocca's book and elsewhere is the one about personalities. Henry Ford is, for better or worse, part of what might be called America's aristocracy. Lee Iacocca wasn't. He was the son of Italian immigrants, a street-wise hustler who worked his way to the top through scholastic brilliance and hard work. It is recorded that Iacocca's openness, chatty repartee, and strong personality needled Ford. He possibly feared Iacocca's charisma, knowing that at any gathering Iacocca would steal the show. For a man with blue blood coursing through his veins, this was perhaps alien to his sensibilities. Worse still, Iacocca's popularity was very high within the company. So Ford got rid of him while the going was good.

So Iacocca had gone, but the '79 Mustang was selling well. It had been selected as the 1979 Indianapolis

500 Pace Car for the second time in its 14-year life, which appeared as a mid-year limited edition package. A non-functional hood scoop, front and rear spoilers, Recaro reclining front seats, and a restyled grille differentiated the "Indy Replica" from other Mustangs. The replica was available only in silver, the lower half painted black with black rear quarter window slats and an attractive red accent stripe. The words "Official Pace Car" were emblazoned in red along the body sides, and the pony reappeared – ponies might be a better description – cantering along the door into the front fenders in subtle gradations from light gray to black.

Little was changed in 1980. Mustang celebrated its 15th anniversary with more refinements than anything else. One option was the attractive diamond-grain, vinyl-covered carriage roof for the notchback. The roof gave the appearance of a convertible with the top up, though a genuine convertible wouldn't appear again until 1984.

Another special model was the Cobra, replete with spoilers like the '79 Pace Car Replica. Essentially, the Cobra was a dress-up kit for the Mustang Turbo with the necessary suspension modifications thrown in. The grille was different from standard Mustangs in that it had two horizontal, down-turned plastic bars in place of the cross-hatch style.

The engine line-up once again offered the four power plants with or without the turbo option. The 200 six now replaced the European V6, which was still in short supply; and the 302 V8 was replaced by a new 255 cid V8 rated at 117 bhp. The reason for this latest – and less powerful – V8 was to enable Ford to comply with CAFE regulations.

Recaro seats were now available on all models, and high-back buckets were standard on the base notchback, but the Ghia models had vinyl buckets with pull-up headrests. As before, the Ghia cars pushed luxury with a vengeance, and door map pockets, roof-mounted assist handles, deluxe steering wheel and a visor vanity mirror, and leather upholstery were offered, the latter in a choice of six colors.

THESE PAGES. One of the Mustang's better models was the GT three-door coupe. It eschewed fake wood for fake brushed aluminum instrument panel trim – and looked better for it. It had excellent cargo space with rear slats folded flat, a 302 V8, Traction Loc limited slip differential, and handling suspension. Costing under $10,000, the GT was a bargain.

THE MUSTANG IMSA

A special Mustang show car was to be seen at auto shows across the country in 1980. It was called the Mustang IMSA, the letters standing for International Motor Sports Association. No other clue was needed: Ford was moving back into racing and was indicating that the IMSA GT series was of particular interest. As for the IMSA showcar, it was a stock Mustang sitting on fat Pirelli tires covered by extremely flared wheel arches. It had a deep front air dam, plastic covers for side windows, head and taillights pop-riveted in place. Its engine was the 140 cid turbo-charged four.

Another interesting race car was the McLaren Mustang introduced during the latter part of 1980. It sat on BBS alloy wheels shod with Firestone 225/SSR-15 radials. The front end lacked a grille, but was equipped with a fat spoiler that extended along the sides of the car. Also included were functional hood scoops, modified suspension, ballooning fender flares, and the turbocharged four. This was fitted with a variable-rate booster to increase output from the stock turbo's 5 psi to 11 psi and completed a very mean-looking racing package. In all, 250 were built, though at $25,000 per car, it's doubtful there were many buyers outside the racetracks.

Times were hard for the motor industry as Mustang entered 1981; sales were suffering a major decline. As for the Mustang itself, it was selling quite well even if it hardly changed from 1979. A few refinements such as reclining back rests became standard, and a T-bar roof style and power windows were additional options for '81. The turbo four could only be specified with manual transmission. An overdrive manual transmission of five speeds was available for the four cylinder engine and had been introduced in mid-1980.

In keeping with Ford's new preoccupation with motor sports, the 302 V8 came bouncing back into the Mustang fold for 1982. Now classed as a high-output engine, the 302 had a special crankshaft, larger carburetor, and a bigger exhaust system. It was available with only a four-speed manual transmission, but in this form was quite capable of pushing Mustang's 0-60 times to between seven and eight seconds. Select-shift automatic transmission, a compulsory option for the six and 255 V8, got a lockup torque converter. Wider wheels and tires were standard on all Mustangs. Due to its poor reliability record, the turbocharged four was dropped and sent back to the drawing board.

Model line-up had increased to six for 1982 and was redesignated with suffixes. L was the standard two-door coupe, followed by a GI two-door coupe. Then in ascending order: GL three-door, GLX two-door, GLX three-door, and finally the ultimate 1982 Mustang, the GT three-door. This came with the 302 HO V8, replacing the Cobra, which slithered away after a long run as the performance Mustang. As with Mustangs since 1979, most changes were refinements such as the larger 15.4-gallon gas tank.

*THESE PAGES. **Costing $3,000 more than the GT coupe, the GT convertible had all the goodies plus wind-in-the-hair driving.***

Sales began to move up again in 1983, much to the industry's relief. Ford chose this year to launch its new aerodynamic shapes onto the market: '82 had seen the Thunderbird, and the compact Tempo was to be announced as an early '84 model.

Mustang continued much as before, again refining an ever-improving product. A new American-built 232 cid (3.8 liter) V6 replaced the aging in-line six in the model line-up. After a year's absence the turbocharged four returned but in modified and much improved form. This engine was available in the GR model, but was distinct from the V8-powered version and was referred to as the Turbo-GT two-door or three-door.

Back in September 1980, Ford announced the formation of its Special Vehicle Operations (SVO) unit. This new department was headed by Michael Kranefuss, who had been imported from his position of competition director of Ford of Europe. Initially SVO developed special cars for competition purposes, but it wasn't too long before Kranefuss and his team developed the truly ultimate Mustang for sale to the public. Three years were to pass before the results of their work finally appeared in the showrooms during the fall of 1983. Announced as a 1984 model, the Mustang SVO had arrived.

THESE PAGES. Some call this the ultimate Mustang. Certainly eye-catching and beautifully styled in current terms, the SVO offers blistering performance from its turbo-charged 140 cid 4-cylinder engine. 0-60 in 7 seconds and 134 mph top speed isn't bad. Four wheel disk brakes and articulated bucket seats with variable lumbar support, performance suspension, and other items make this $15,600 car a driving experience on a par with European sport machinery. Note the source of the SVO's performance, the turbo-charged 2-3 liter (140 cid) 4-cylinder engine.

THE SVO ULTIMATE

Without a doubt the best looking post-1979 Mustang to come down the turnpike, the SVO is a true thoroughbred. Powered by a throttle-body, fuel–injected turbocharged SOHC four, rated at 145 bhp, the SVO proved to be as fast as, if not faster than, the V8-powered GT.

The turbocharger is equipped with an intercooler, a novel device which drops the air intake temperature from 300°F to 175°F resulting in a 20 percent power boost. Electronic controls automatically adjust the turbo boost at any given situation. The 0-60 time is around 7.5 seconds and top speed is 130 mph. Remember the huge 428 V8s powering 1969 Mustangs? What a far cry from those brute force and ignorance days. Imagine a massive V8 hard put to whip this little four!

Four-wheel disk brakes, Koni adjustable shocks all around, a superb suspension system, and a five-speed manual transmission made the Mustang SVO one of the most roadworthy cars in the world. It was – and is – a very European-looking automobile with its no-grille front with a massive functional hoodscoop, flared wheel arches, and 225/50VR-16 Goodyear NCT tires on 7-inch aluminum wheels. Articulated bucket seats with adjustable lumbar support are standard, with leather upholstery as an option. This latterday car is a cut above the rest.

The model line-up for 1984 recalled the heady days of the late Sixties with no less than 10 variations to choose

from. One was the convertible, introduced in 1983, in three versions: the LX, GT, and Turbo GT. A new, smaller grille with a rectangular crosshatch theme was the first really noticeable design change since 1979. Turn-signal lights flash yellow at the rear, though this feature, adopted in Europe years ago, had been on Mustangs since the third-generation cars were introduced. In the case of blinker lights, all that has to be done is jiggle the wiring a little and replace red lenses with amber ones. A number of U.S. cars now have this feature, but not every make has adopted it. Five engine variations were on offer for 1984. These consisted of the base SOHC in-line four rated at 88 bhp, the turbo-charged four rated at 145 bhp, an ohv V6, and two V8s rated at 165 and 175 bhp each. The last two engines were very potent units capable of rapid acceleration times, along with a top speed approaching 130 mph. It does sometimes seem pointless, though, to build cars with high top speeds – the Corvette, for example, can go to 160 plus – when the speed limit is only 55–65.

The SVO continued in 1985 with minor improvements, including a horsepower increase to 175. According to one prestigious automotive journal, the SVO could out-handle both the Porsche 944 and Ferrari 308. Again, it was a matter of minor modifications; Ford seemed content to leave the model alone – the Corvette kept the same body for 14 years, the Camaro for almost as long.

Another view of a thoroughbred: the ultimate Mustang SVO

Twenty years separate these two; one is a 1965, the other a 1985. Bearing in mind the philosophies behind the two, which would you rather have? A 5.0-liter (302 cid) V8 powers the '85 GT, which has handling to match.

THESE PAGES. Photographed outside
Ford's World Headquarters Building
in Dearborn, a 1985 SVO. Fewer
than 3,000 were built in '85.

*THESE PAGES. **The sleek 1985 GT 5.0.***

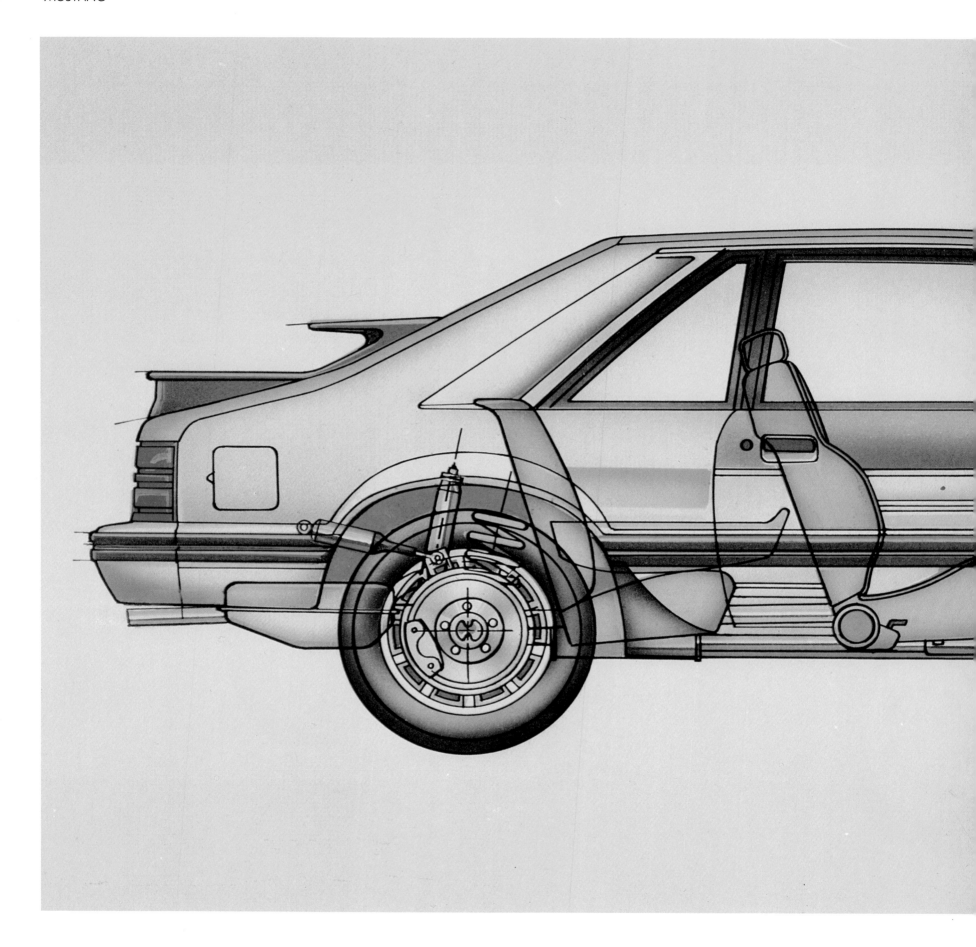

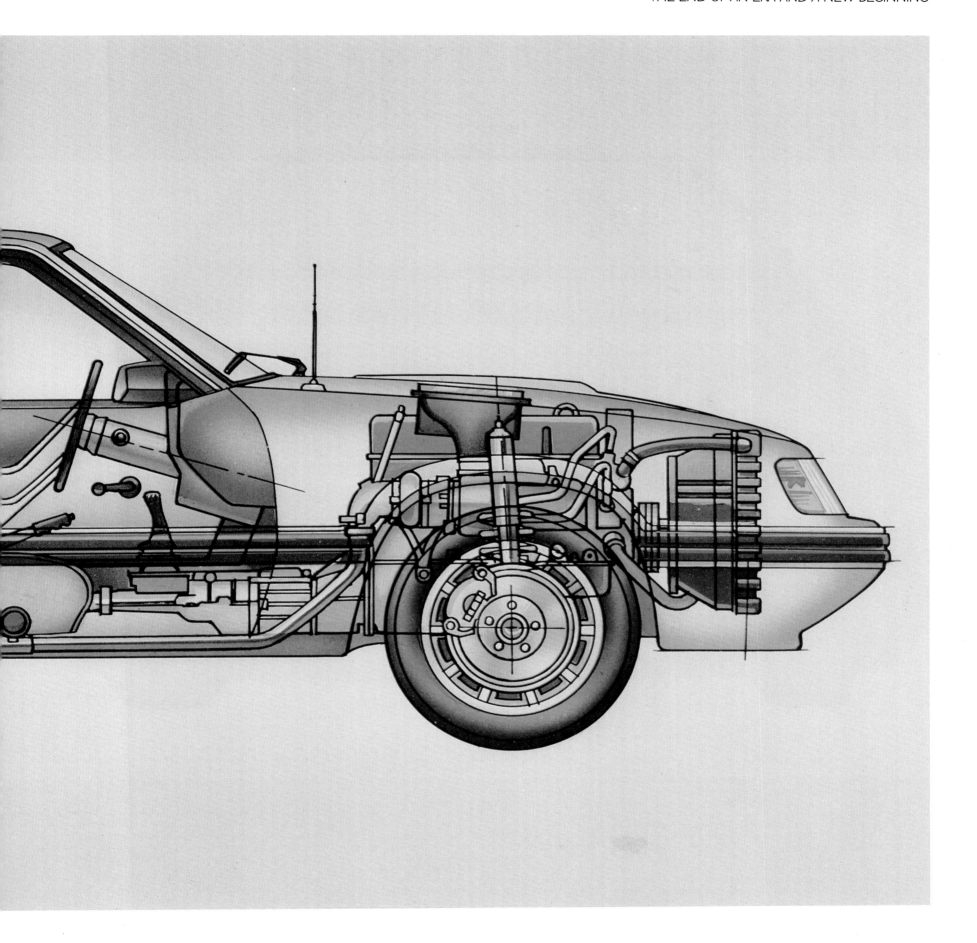

Cutaway rendering of the 1985 SVO gives some idea of what makes it tick.

ABOVE AND RIGHT. The rear view of this '85 shows unique placement of the federally mandated extra stoplight. The engine is the raunchy turbocharged 4 found in the SVO which has become something of a cult. Surprisingly poor sales meant 1986 was the SVO's last year. This Mustang is a sure-fire collectible, so grab it while you can, as numbers were limited.

MUSTANGS FOR 1986

In 1986, Mustang again raced forward with no major — or minor, for that matter — revisions apart from those not visible to the naked eye. The high-output V8 with four-barrel carburetor became an engine of the past as Mustang finally embraced fuel injection on the V8s. Only the LX's standard 2.3-liter OHC four remained with a carburetor, though the LX convertible eschewed the four banger in favor of a throttle-bodied fuel injection system on its 120 horse V6.

As for the SVO, it always had fuel injection. 1986 improvements included a horsepower increase to 205 at 5000 rpm. While the SVO was technically more advanced than the 200 horsepower V8-powered GT, it was the latter most buyers wanted.

As always, the options list was enormous. It included three- and four-speed automatic transmissions, the latter an overdrive unit, as was the five-speed manual. A four-speed manual was standard on the four-cylinder LX. There was a flip-up removable sunroof, air conditioning, console with clock and graphics monitor, leather articulated sport seats, power locks, tinted windows, premium sound system, the list went on and on.

1986 was to be the refreshing SVO's final year in production. Ford had weighed the pros and cons and decided that what the market wanted was Sixties-style V8 power. Although the SVO would be gone, the new GT to come would cannibalize much of the former's suspension. It looked as though real performance was finally going to make a comeback.

The 1986 Mustang SVO had changed little since its 1984 birth. From the third-generation model's beginning in 1979, Mustang emerged as an engineering tour de force with the manners of a true thoroughbred.

7

IT SNORTS, IT BELLOWS, THE MUSTANG GALLOPS ONCE MORE

Or should this chapter be called "the Mustang came roaring back?" Thanks to Mike Kranefuss, who used to run Ford's European racing program before he was transferred to Dearborn to oversee the Special Vehicle Operations, and gifted engineer Jack Roush, Ford recognized that what had been done with the SVO could also be done with the 5.0-liter GT. The shame was the axing of the SVO because Americans liked to think power only came from a V8. "There's no substitute for cubic inches" used to be the clarion call. So Ford gave them back cubic inches, albeit disguised as liters.

The 1987 Mustang, though still wearing its 1979 suit of clothes, was an admirable redesign from the angular shape of before to a more rounded, aerodynamic profile that was the corporate identity. Most of the change was at the front, and now the car had no grille. Flush-fitting headlights were adopted from the late SVO, there was a large air-scoop under the front bumper, and a bunch of macho adornments such as front and rear fender scoops, sills, and a rear spoiler. This stuff only came on the GT, not the LX, which was staid by comparison.

Under the hood was the familiar 4.9-liter block... or 50 cc shy of the 5.0 liters to which everybody, including Ford, who slapped 5.0-liter badges on the sides, commonly refer. Horsepower was rated at 200 in 1986; now it was 225 at 4,200 rpm. With this extra power, the use of much of the SVO's front suspension such as plastic ball joints, caster changes that reduce camber,

superior anti-roll bar mountings, and modified MacPherson struts with the springs mounted separately on the lower arms, were adopted to good effect.

It has rack and pinion steering with a fast 2.2 turns lock to lock, and its very sporty, ergonomically designed interior has European flair, probably because it was designed by the same man, Trevor Creed, who put together the Merkur interior. Legible white-on-black numbers adorn the instrument panel directly in front of the driver, who has no trouble viewing them through the well-placed steering wheel. The seats were well-designed for comfort and even had lumbar adjustments. Large 15-inch wheels shod in P225/60VR-15 gatorbacks helped no end in terms of ride and handling.

Everybody liked the '87. Car magazines gave it high marks for performance, handling and finish. One magazine managed a top speed of over 144 mph, while another said with different gearing it was good for 150. And by the way, 0 to 60 came in just over six seconds. All this could be had for a bargain price of $14,150 or thereabouts.

We have been talking about the GT coupe, but there was also a GT convertible which was a little more expensive. Lower down the order came the LX with an OHC EFI four-cylinder engine as standard. The V6 had been dropped after 1986. However, the LX was available with the big V8 minus the spoilers, scoops, and rear air foil.

Total sales for 1987 were 163,592, down from the previous year's 175,000-plus. The following year, there

LEFT. *This striking yellow convertible was a 1993 limited-edition feature car produced to bolster sales for and old design.*

ABOVE. *The 1992 Mustang convertible was the way to travel on a sultry summer evening. The 5.0-liter V8 gave out plenty of punch.*

was a decent improvement even though the car was virtually identical to the '87. Ford let it be known that this body style would be around for at least three more years, which made Mustang buffs very happy.

There had been rumors that the 1987 car was to be smaller, lighter... and Japanese. The outcry was enormous, surprising even Ford who received thousands upon thousands of letters pleading for the Mustang to remain entirely American. From its conception, the Mustang had been a truly all-American sporty car, an exclusively American car, so it was, as far as Mustang lovers were concerned, the work of traitors if it became a front-wheel-drive sports car built by the Japanese. Which, if the truth be told, is exactly what Ford intended to do.

After much consideration, Ford decided to keep the Mustang as an all-American car. This was the right decision, not only for the Mustang, but for Ford as well. Had the company not taken any notice of its followers, there is little doubt sales would have been seriously affected on all Ford products. Instead the new sporty car, code-named ST16, was christened the Probe, and not a moment too soon. Just six months before its introduction, the car was going to be the new Mustang and even had the name stamped on the bumper. That's how close Ford came to ending an American success story.

Whatever the circumstances, the Probe has become a great success in its own right and has a decidedly loyal following. It is good enough to have won the prestigious *Motor Trend* Car of the Year Award and is as American as it could possibly be, considering its origins are in the Land of the Rising Sun. Today the Probe is entirely built in Flat Rock, Michigan, though it shares its mechanical components with the Mazda MX-6. The styling, however, is unique to the Probe.

There really was no difference between the 1987 and 1988 Mustangs. Both the LX and GT came in coupe and convertible form. As before, the standard LX power plant was the little 2.3-liter overhead cam four. The 225 hp V8 was optional on the LX, standard on the GT which had

no other power plant. Sales of the '88 jumped 50,000 over the previous year; whether this was a reflection of customer loyalty after the "Made in Japan" scare, nobody quite knows.

Eight years of Ronald Reagan's tenure at the White House had finally come to an end. As the Hollywood cowboy rode off into the sunset to his millionaire's ranch dragging Reaganomics behind him, George Bush stepped into the breech to face, among other things, the legacy of the Savings and Loan scandal.

Ford had worries of its own – not problems that would require immediate attention, but problems that would have to be faced if there was to be a 1994 Mustang. Government regulations targeted 1994 as the year when all cars would require driver's and passenger's airbags. Ford would either have to make a considerable financial commitment or face the emotional responsibility of having to kill off an institution.

Designers, product planners, engineers, and marketing men met in the corridors and talked about the Mustang; they had lunches and talked about the Mustang, got together in respective offices or studios... and talked about the Mustang. They would feed their ideas to Program Manager Ken Dabrowski who, being sympathetic with their cause, evolved the group into a "skunkworks" team. Skunkworks, by the way, means a small group of skilled people who put together a project in the shortest possible time. With such a team in place, any competitors could effectively be "skunked," and the project could be brought to fruition first. But what if the opposition has a skunkworks team as well...

While the Skunkworks team designed and discussed what should be done to save American's favorite Pony from the chop, Ford unveiled the 1989 Mustang. There wasn't a great deal to see as the Mustang was concerned; apart from minor differences, it was just the same as the year before, and the year before that. And what differences there were consisted of the GT's articulated front seats in the LX, power windows and door locks

BELOW. The "plasticky" interior wasn't the traditional idea of a grand touring package in the old European sense, but it was a lot safer. By 1989 the 5.0-liter engine was becoming quite familiar.

made standard on the convertibles, and LX models ordered with the 5.0L V8 picked up a new emblem which was designated LX 5.0L Sport.

NO BIRTHDAY PARTY

Everybody thought that, since 1989 was Mustang's 25th anniversary, Ford was sure to bring out a special limited edition model. Oddly, and for reasons only Ford knew about, no anniversary car was forthcoming. With the very real probability that Mustang might be nearing the end of the road anyway, and with nobody really knowing what decisions would be reached, a special edition might have appeared a triviality.

Still no decision had been reached by the middle of the summer as to whether the Mustang was to survive or not. As if oblivious to the controversy it was causing, the

1990 Mustang was meeting the press at Ford's annual long lead program. Long lead, by the way, is the term used by auto manufacturers to describe the event which allows the media to see the following year's models several months before they go on sale.

Once again, it was a case of déjà vu; the 1990 car was identical to the previous year's model. Small but significant items such as driver's air bag were part of the 1990 package. To accommodate the air bag, which was housed in the steering wheel hub, the tilt steering column was deleted.

By September 1989 the Skunkworks Team, headed by engineering design manager for Mustang, John Coletti, reported it would be possible to design and build a brand new Mustang with a far smaller financial investment than had been thought realistic. What Skunkworks

BELOW. Late '80s machismo was the name of the game for the Mustang GT, but it struck a vulgar, unsophisticated note. All the spoilers, scoops and ground-effects did little or nothing for performance. The standard V8-powered LX without add-ons was just as fast, and more attractive.

BELOW. *The small airfoil on this 1992 LX is mainly for show.*

ABOVE. *The pudgy steering hub hides an air-bag – an excellent safety feature no car should be without.*

wanted in return was a commitment from management to establish what is now known as a "collocated/dedicated" team that would work only on the Mustang and nothing else. They would require their own building where all the Mustang team members would work without interference from other projects. This was a revolutionary approach to the problems of car design. Instead of creating a new car while working on others, as was the traditional way, collocated/dedicated (working in one place and only on the Mustang) would have the advantage of speed brought about by a streamlined and efficient operation that would ultimately save money.

It took another 11 months before the idea came to fruition. During that time, the Skunkworks team continued their everyday jobs, working on the Mustang project without pay at night. By this time Scots-born Alex Trotman, who among other things had been head of product planning for Ford of Europe during the Sixties, was brought over from Great Britain to take over as Executive Vice-President of Ford North American Automotive Operations. Fortunately for Skunkworks, Trotman was in favor of the Mustang. He reviewed what had been done so far and asked that the team should adopt a "fresh-eyes" approach to the new-generation model which should be built at an affordable price.

Trotman's experiences with sporty cars in Europe qualified him to understand the Mustang program. He knew at

first hand the sorts of problems associated with projects such as this, having already been heavily involved with Ford's sporty Capri, Europe's "Mini-Mustang." During the Sixties, before Dearborn had finally decided on the 1965½ Mustang, Trotman had brought to the U.S.A. a running prototype of the Capri. He had hoped that the Capri would become the new Mustang instead of the Dearborn concept. Now the boot was on the other foot; he was trying to save it. "The Mustang is an icon," he said. "We must invest in the car because it is the right thing to do."

With encouragement like this, the Skunkworks team felt that their labors would not be in vain. Every Thursday, the team would meet at 4 P.M. in Building Number Three of the Engineering Center. Here the team would lay out ideas, plan strategy, sometimes not leaving until nine in the evening.

While all this was going on, Ford announced a special Limited Edition Mustang to try and boost flagging 1990 sales. It was a convertible decked out in Emerald Jewel Green Metallic Clearcoat paint, with a white top and white leather interior. Really a dressed-up 5.0-liter LX convertible, the Limited Edition hit the road at $19,878. It didn't stop the sales slide from an '89 total of over 209,000 to slightly over 128,000. The writing was on the wall; the country was heading for a recession. Still, owners will be happy to know only 3,837 Emerald Jewel

Green Limited Editions were built.

One reason that Mustang sales took a nosedive could simply be that the car had grown stale. The same body had been around for 11 years and had been honed and refined almost as far as it would go. There were three seasons left with the current body. Decisions were needed, new directions to follow. It was going to be very difficult to convince Ford chiefs that the Mustang should be saved, especially when the Probe and the all-new Thunderbird were doing so well in the specialty market.

New 16-inch alloy wheels distinguished 1991 V8 powered Mustangs, and the four-cylinder models got a more powerful 2.3-liter engine boasting two spark plugs per cylinder. Horsepower got a boost from the new cylinder head to 105 from the previous year's 88. A new shift lock on automatic transmission models meant the brake pedal had to be depressed to shift out of Park. And a new paint color was offered; 1990's Limited Edition Deep Emerald Jewel Green Metallic. Combined with the same interior and exterior fittings, the car is identical to the 1990 special. But there is a giveaway for the eagle-eyed: 1990 had 15-inch wheels; 1991 had 16 inches. The emerald green paint wasn't available after 1991, thus leaving a suspicion that Ford hadn't used it all up in 1990!

The 1992 and 1993 models were again exactly the

THESE PAGES. After 13 years with the same body and platform, the 1992 Mustang was becoming a little long in the tooth. An all-new Mustang was still two years away. The 1992 GT looks at home on the drag strip, though the engine would need coaxing to make it a worthy quarter-miler. Nonetheless, it was an excellent sportscar for the money, its 5.0-liter, H.O. V8 having more than enough power for everyday use.

Only 1,419 yellow Limited Edition special convertibles were built in 1993. This model and a special white Limited Edition convertible (1,460 built) were Ford's way of giving the last of the third-generation Mustangs a cheery send-off. There would be an all-performance Cobra in mid-'93 but this yellow convertible really closes a Mustang chapter.

same, though after a dismal 1992 production year of only 79,000 units, Ford cranked out a few more specials. In 1992 buyers had the choice of a Limited Edition car painted Vibrant Red. Special features included a white convertible top with ebony headliner, Opal pearlescent 16-inch GT wheels, unique rear deck spoiler, impractical and rather vulgar white leather seating with black piping, and a package named PEP 245A which supplied a power equipment group, cruise control, and electronic premium sound AM/FM cassette radio. All the buyer needed was an extra $850 and the Limited Edition model was his/hers... if there were enough available, that is. Actually only 2,196 were made of this model, guaranteeing owners won't see another like theirs too often.

By the time the 1993 models were announced, it looked as though the recession had finally run out of steam. Car sales began moving back onto a healthy course, and a new President with new ideas was making himself felt at the White House. As for Mustang, it was much the same diet once again, though this time everybody knew the 14-year-old body was in its final year.

A pair of Limited Edition models were issued this time, a ploy used to milk as much out of the old body as possi-

BELOW. Even the attractive color can't hide the massive front end, though the interior is nicely thought-out (bottom). The grille (center) is simple and effective, while the engine (bottom right) is not one for the D.I.Y. enthusiast to work on!

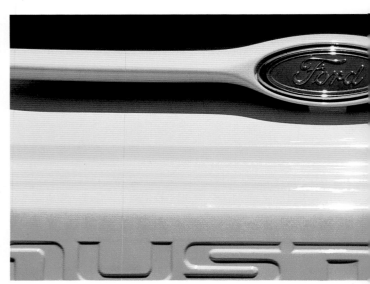

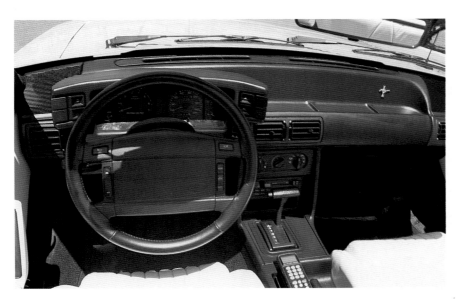

ble. The Feature Cars were either all-white with matching white leather seats, color-keyed 16 x 7 inch wheels, and black front floor mats with black pony embroidery, or more strikingly, yellow with black or white leather interior, a yellow pony stitched on the black floor mats, and chrome plated 16-inch wheels. Both cars also had black-on-black or white-on-white ponies embroidered on the front seat headrests. Numbers were very small: 1,460 White LX Convertibles and 1,419 Yellow ones.

Revised horsepower measurements adjusted the previous 225 to 205... there was actually no difference, only a more accurate measurement. The V8-powered '93s were just as quick, just as powerful. But not as powerful as Mustang's last hurrah with the old body. In mid-season, shortly after the Feature Cars, Ford unveiled a ferocious new Cobra. The product of the recently formed Special Vehicles Team, the Cobra was no slouch. With 235 horsepower under the hood, the car invoked memories of the late Sixties, though with much more precision and better handling and ride. The 16-inch wheels shod in low-profile tires helped minimize wheel-spin, but all that power up front was unforgiving on mildly damp surfaces.

Then the tail would twitch and the wheels would spin, but would soon be back under control.

Four thousand nine hundred and ninety-three Cobras were built, and it proved a popular seller. The car was so hot that road-test journalists had no fewer than eight Cobras stolen from beneath their feet. It was a good car, though, eclipsing the brand-new Pontiac Firebird and Chevrolet Camaro, both of which were faster than the stock Mustang GT. Another attention grabber to pull interest away from the GM ponies was the special Mustang III concept car. Shown simultaneously at the Detroit International Motor Show and the Los Angeles exhibit, the Mustang III created a lot of interest.

Sales for 1993 were 35,000 better than 1992. The economy was moving again. Everybody knew once Ford finally gave the go-ahead for a 30th Anniversary, all-new Mustang soon to burst upon the world's auto stage. A steady build-up of publicity, from "leaked" information, spy photographs, magazine articles, and all the usual come-ons that precede a new car launch, made absolutely sure that nobody would be unaware of Mustang's second coming.

*BOTTOM LEFT. **The pony stitched on the seats was exclusive to Limited Edition models though the aerofoil (below) was available on standard 5.0-liter models.***

8
MUSTANG'S
RENAISSANCE

December 8, 1993. Winter had spread its icy chill earlier than usual, forewarning the Northeast and Midwest of much worse to follow. But December 8, 1993 was also the day when the all-new Mustang went on sale at dealers across the country. Brightly colored shorts worn with white tennis shoes walked across Florida showroom floors; out West it was jeans and pretty blouses. Wrapped up in heavy winter coats, hats, boots and scarves, Northern souls braved leaden skies, snow flurries, and slippery pavements to make their first acquaintance with the brand new car.

As we have already seen, the 1994 Mustang nearly didn't happen. And wouldn't have happened had it not been for the dedication of John Coletti's Skunkworks team. They knew the car had to be a front-engine, rear-drive car with V8 power and plenty of muscle. That's what the thousands of Mustang enthusiasts wanted... it had to be a traditional all-American pony car.

In August 1989, the Skunkworks team was put together. It consisted of nine talented Ford people. By September the team had a plan of operation. Next would come a clay model and a business plan which told how much the project would cost. This would be presented to Alex Trotman for his approval.

Work began on the first clay model in November 1989. John Coletti and fellow team member, Ronald Muccioli, whose role was planning within the group, asked another Skunkworks team member, designer John Aiken, to style a clay model as fast as possible. The brief

was for the car to be uniquely different from the "jellybean" look that had been so fashionable since the revolutionary Taurus initially made its bow.

John Aiken started designing cars for Ford in 1959 and even contributed to the first Mustang. His task now was to fashion something for the backroom boys, the clay modelers who are normally never mentioned, to work on. Eventually there would be three clays for evaluation; the Bruce Jenner, the Arnold Schwarzenegger, and the Rambo. Jenner was a great Olympic decathlon champion; the other two were names of the most violent men in movies, apparently to convey aggressive masculinity because Skunkworks wanted a muscle-car image built into the new Mustang. Funny, isn't it? When the Mustang name was originally chosen, the last thing Ford wanted was an aggressive, warlike image associated with the World War II fighter of the same name. As the world knows, some bright spark looked in the dictionary and discovered mustang ponies. Problem solved.

My, how times have changed.

A clay model with Skunkworks team design parameters was proposed by Aiken and built by the clay modelers. It was shown to Trotman, who was delighted with the progress. Up to that point, the limited finance available to Skunkworks was coming from Coletti's budget. Trotman asked what the team needed. Three more months to work out all the details, was the reply.

Skunkworks put together a complete strategy... from marketing to car measurements... along with the overall cost. Next came the clays. Working from a secret studio

Aiken produced the Jenner clay. When shown the Jenner, Skunkworks wasn't entirely happy, deeming it not aggressive enough. At this point, the team commissioned the California Clay, which was sculpted by the California Concept Center. Then both finished clays were taken to Pomona, California, where Mustang enthusiasts had the chance to give their opinion. There the Jenner design won easily.

Still not happy, the team initiated steps for two further designs. In late summer of 1990, Ford set up a competition between two design teams to come up with a more aggressive shape than the ones already submitted. On October 18, 1990, both the Jenner and Rambo designs were displayed in the Ford Design Center. At the same time, a fiberglass copy of Rambo was sent to California for enthusiast reaction.

Rambo was deemed too radical for production; in late October, the Schwarzenegger clay was put on display and a copy sent out to San Jose, California. From Dearborn to San Jose, Schwarzenegger was declared the winner; this was to be the new Mustang. Corporate approval was swift; now the real work would begin to develop and engineer it ready for production.

As for the Skunkworks team, their job was done. They had revolutionized the conception, design, and execution of a new car project. A small band of individuals all working together on the same project instead of doing it piecemeal... one day the Mustang, the next the Taurus... had achieved much in far less time, at less cost, and using fewer human resources. Now it was time to hand over to another group called Team Mustang headed by Program Manager Will Boddie. The group's job

FAR LEFT. Team Mustang created this show car to what appetites for the fourth generation car soom soon to follow. Called Mustang III, the car style the new 1993 Camaro and Firebird's thunder when it was unveiled.

THIS PAGE. The appropriately named "Rambo" design (top left) was considered too aggressive while the "Bruce Jenner" (top right) was thought to be too meek. Just right was the "Schwarzenegger" (left), pictured with master modeller Cicel Crider.
ABOVE. Interior designer Emeline King created the 1994 model's dashboard.

was to turn a dream into reality, to develop the car ready for production. The team was given 37 months to bring the concept to fruition.

In today's cut-throat global automobile market, timing is of the essence to stay ahead of the game. Any delays means somebody else will get there first. Ford, who has been streamlining its operations with great success over the past few years, inaugurated a new way to bring new models to market faster than the traditional 48-to-54 months it normally takes. This new process is called World Class Timing (WCT).

The 1994 Mustang was the first program to use WCT, and it worked. WCT is rather like countdown to a space launch; the program begins "T-minus-35," then each stage of development is monitored to the conclusion, when the first car comes off the line... or "blast off," as they would call it at Mission Control!

World Class Timing was developed by Ford personnel from North American Automotive Operations. They became known as the 411 Team because they operated out of Room 411 of a Ford office building. For over a year, the 411 Team reviewed and reblended every stage of a new vehicle's development. The program was broken down into segments called "disciplines," which referred to design, engineering, manufacturing, marketing, and so on. Ken Kohrs, vice-president of Car Product Development, says understanding and refining processes are essential to WCT.

"They understand the process they are working on," says Kohrs. "They use that process with intense discipline. They focus their resources on the deliverables, on getting the job done."

As mentioned earlier, Team Mustang was placed under one roof... they took up residence in Allen Park, a Detroit suburb adjacent to Dearborn. Here, an old warehouse had been converted into a technical center.

"A fundamental element of World Class Timing is to have the people who make the decisions housed together with the people who execute those decisions on a daily basis," said Mike Zevalkink, who took over as Mustang Program manager when Will Boddie became Director of Small and Midsize Car Segment.

"They participate in those discussions on a daily basis," Zevalkink went on. "And even if the final decision isn't their first choice, they understand the tradeoffs and constraints that shaped it. They own or buy into the decisions a lot better than when you're trying to communicate from one building to another, one city to another, or one organizational chimney to another." More or less, that is what WCT is all about. By the end, WCT had proved its worth; the $700 million Mustang project saved almost 30 percent in overall costs while improving quality of product at the same time. In fact, the program was completed in 35 months, eight weeks ahead of schedule.

Many think the 1994 Mustang is new from the ground up, but it isn't. The car still uses the Fox platform that has been with Mustang since 1979, albeit with a number of important modifications which improved the handling and ride. Another thing: the rear axle is the same as before.

There's nothing wrong with the Fox chassis; when Team Mustang started to develop the car, they found their chassis design was almost identical to what had gone before. So, rather than start from a clean sheet of paper, the engineers decided it would not only be simpler, but also more cost-effective, to modify the existing Fox platform to suit.

Called the FOX-4 chassis for the '94 car, the engineers made it much stronger and less inclined to flex under hard usage such as fast cornering. Many might think a stiffer chassis will mean a rough ride; fortunately, this is not the case. By strengthening the cowl area, door posts, the base of the hinge post, a section at the back of the B-pillar, and finally the box sections, the engineers succeeded in producing a vastly superior-handling car without any of the discomfort associated with vehicles of front-engine, live-rear axle design.

"We really emphasized body rigidity," said Will Boddie who was Program Manager from 1990 until 1993. A stiffer body gives the engineers more leeway to tune the chassis and make it behave the way they want it to under varying conditions. People will notice the difference most, Boddie claimed, on rough road surfaces where "it in no way resembles the '93 car."

Boddie was insistent that the FOX-4 was not "a carryover platform. The car behaves very well, even at its limits. It's a more-developed, friendly car than its competitors. It's more refined." And perhaps to make sure the media didn't think the FOX-4 platform was old hat, Ford dished out a series of photographs showing the Mustang body and platform painted red and white. All that was new was painted red. Only the floorpan, which received minor modifications, was painted white. In fact, of the 1,850 platform parts, 1,330 are new.

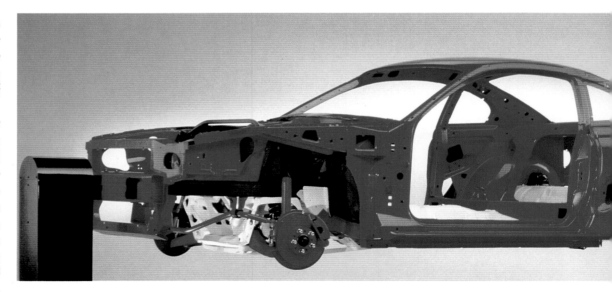

ABOVE. Significant changes to Mustang's Fox platform made it almost totally new. Everything colored red is new; only the white parts are carry-overs. Yellow is the convertible only, while blue parts are modified from the previous model.
TOP. The winning "Schwarzenegger" design.
RIGHT. Cutaway view of Mustang's base V6 which has 40 bhp more than the previous in-line 4.

Other major differences between the '94 and its predecessors included a 3.7-inch wider track (on the six-cylinder models, 1.9 inches wider on the GT), a 0.75-inch longer wheelbase, new front suspension geometry, increased structural rigidity, four wheel disk brakes as standard, with ABS as an option.

A new 3.8-liter V6 developing 145 horsepower replaced the old four-banger unit as Mustang's basic power plant. Actually, the engine is not that new; it has been powering Taurus to Continental cars for some time. However, it is a very versatile, willing workhorse with a surprising amount of snap. Sequential port fuel-injection and a new EEC-V engine management system help the engine's efficiency and economy, while its lusty 215 lb-ft of torque developed at 2,500 rpm, mated to the manual five-speed transmission, pulls the car along at a very healthy pace. Nobody need be ashamed of owning a V6-powered Mustang any more.

Of course, most people will prefer the V8, the quintessential American power plant guaranteed to put hair on a newborn baby's chest. In the case of the new Mustang GT, it certainly will, for the engine is capable of 0 to 60 times in 6.5 seconds and 140 mph plus.

The engine's heritage goes back as far as the Mustang itself, farther in fact. It was part of Ford's new small block series in 1962 and had a 221-cubic-inch displacement, but was stroked to 260 not long after. The first V8-powered '64½ Mustangs had the 260 block. In September 1964, the 260 was stroked again to become the world-famous 289 which powered not only Mustangs, but sports and racing cars. This engine won the Le Mans 24-hour endurance race twice, in 1968 and again in 1969, this time stroked to the now-familiar 302 or 5.0-liter displacement.

Because the 1994 Mustang's profile is too low to accommodate the 302 used in previous models, Team Mustang decided upon the unit used in the current Thunderbird and Cougar models. A lineal descendant of the original small block V8, the engine fitted neatly under the hood of the new car. Initially, there were a couple of problems; the engine had to be moved forward 0.75 inch to fit "four into two" catalytic converters. These have more volume than the ones on the '93 cars. This was fine, but moving the engine forward to accommodate the converters meant there was no room for a cooling fan for the radiator. The answer: An electric fan that had the added advantage of not causing horsepower loss as the normal engine-driven unit would. As far as the engine's horsepower rating was concerned, the engineers raised it from the 195 found in the Thunderbird to a healthy 215 in the Mustang.

Underneath the Mustang is a fairly familiar suspension layout consisting of a modified MacPherson strut system in the front with the coil springs placed between the front crossmember (which was moved forward for '94) and lower control arms which are slightly longer than before to improve steering and suspension geometries. The front caster has been increased from 1.5 to 4 degrees to improve Mustang's directional stability.

At the rear, the age-old rigid axle has been lifted intact from the '93 Mustang. It is located by four trailing links, and the coil springs are positioned between the body and lower links. An interesting specification are the four shock absorbers. Two are positioned normally, while the other two are mounted horizontally to prevent axle wind-up during wild and wooly acceleration. There are anti-roll bars front and rear which are standard on all models.

Anybody taking a look at the latest Fourth-Generation Mustang can see a car that is eminently qualified to be driven into the 21st century. According to Program Manager Mike Zevalkink, the likelihood of any structural changes or body redesign is minimal. Yes, Ford's excellent overhead cam, modular V8 will find its way under the hood in the not-too-distant future, probably in dual-overhead-cam form. Apart from evolutionary improvements, there is really nothing to be done.

In a sense the 1994 Mustang can be described as a "Rebirth." While it doesn't look anything like the 1964½ model, there's no mistaking the lineage. But nostalgia has been designed into the shape, the recognizable side scoops, the left-facing galloping pony in the grille, the almost-fastback roofline and short rear deck all hark back thirty years to the first Mustang.

"If you really analyze this car," said Bud Magaldi, Mustang Design Manager since 1990, "there's an awful lot of the '64½ and 1965 car in there. Just look at the new car, the way it was done with the character lines on the body side, the horses and the long hood. Yet it is contemporary."

According to Magaldi, the car was designed with the help of the public. As we saw earlier, three clays were shown to the public at "consumer clinics" across the country, beginning in 1989. The winning car was the one with the side scoops, the pony, etc. "The people we interviewed wanted galloping horses on the car," Magaldi said. "But they also said that, even if you took all the horses off, the car should still look like a Mustang."

And it did.

Taking the people's favorite, the Schwarzenegger car, the design team, which numbered 40 members at one point, created the design which became the production Mustang.

"When we finished," recalled Magaldi, "we talked to enthusiasts individually to get their candid comments. Then we asked them collectively, 'What do you think?'

"Well, they stood up and applauded. They gave the car a standing ovation. That was quite a surprise. We were really happy with that."

"By having a rich history, the Mustang provided us with dozens of styling accents..." Emeline King, Interior Designer for the Mustang, smiled somewhat shyly, yet there was no hiding the pride that beamed from her large, brown eyes. Emeline had a right to be proud, because her yesterday/today/tomorrow interior design took some beating. From the previous, rather angular design, Ms. King cleverly took the old dual cockpit theme and returned the pony to the steering wheel, yet created a passenger compartment of flowing, rounded lines and

shapes that say continuity. Seats are ergonomic; certainly the best Mustang has ever had. The double cowl dashboard has nice rounded instruments, and driver and passenger air bags are standard.

"An interior design succeeds if it complements the exterior design," Emeline King. "A lot of the Mustang cues that are occurring on the exterior have been incorporated into the interior, so it becomes a single, unified design." Ms. King is absolutely correct; the unity of line and function is seldom as obvious as on the new Mustang.

Two months ahead of schedule, Team Mustang's job was finished; the 1994 Mustang was ready for production. Then the car undertook a series of tests to make sure everything would be right when production started on October 1, 1993.

An interesting aside to the Mustang story is the Mustang III. While Team Mustang was still more than a year away from completion, Mustang Business Planning Manager John Coletti heard arch rivals Chevrolet and Pontiac would be launching the all-new Camaro and Firebird at the 1993 Detroit and Los Angeles car shows. Knowing that the pair of GM ponies were attractive enough to steal the shows, Coletti decided to steal some of their thunder too, by revising an old Ford tradition of displaying a highly stylized concept car which would have strong hints of the production Mustang to come.

Perched on whopping 19-inch wheels, the Mustang III show car more than achieved its objective. It created a huge amount of interest, even more than Coletti could have dreamed. The III was no cobbled-together nonrunner; it was a practical, fully equipped driving vehicle powered by a 4.6-liter 4-cam V8. Touches such as a Roots-type blower and air-to-ethylene-glycol intercooler help push horsepower from 280 to 450. A six-speed manual Borg-Warner transmission – the same as the Viper and new Camaro/Firebird – takes power via the aluminum driveshaft to the rigid rear axle.

On the inside of the Mustang III, Emeline King's handiwork is immediately evident. In fact, the III's two-tone interior was very close to the production Mustang.

Ford continued to promote the Mustang III throughout the spring and summer of 1993. At Ford's early preview of 1994 cars, the Mustang III was much in evidence. So too were prototypes of the production Mustang, which teased the assembled journalists by driving around the proving track disguised in zebra-style black stripes to prevent anyone from getting a serious look. A few months later, it became a game with drivers on I-94, the Chicago-to-Detroit highway, to see how close they could get to the many new Mustangs being driven along there almost every day.

Ford's big tease was the beautiful Mustang III show car, pictured here at Ford's proving ground in 1993.

THESE PAGES. *The honeycomb scoops (above), a modular 4.6-liter 4 cam V8 engine (right) and the exterior styling all signal a powerful package.*

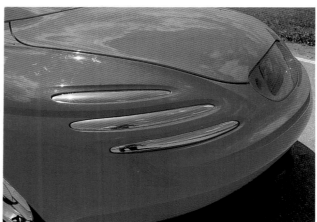

The sleek styling and interior by designer Emeline King made the Mustang III a dream that, with only a little modification, could become a reality for drivers everywhere.

Driving the 1994 Mustang was an experience in itself. It is as different from the '93 car as can be imagined. The car comes as two models, the base Mustang and the performance-pounding GT. Two bodystyles, a coupe and convertible, are offered on both models. An interesting option on the convertible is the removable hardtop roof with full headlining. The roof can be taken off and put back on easily by two people. A storage bag and stand for the roof when it is not in use are provided.

Standard transmission on both the Mustang and GT is the five-speed manual with an electronic four-speed automatic offered as an option. It goes without saying that performance-minded buyers will stick to the manual, which is superior to many European and Japanese boxes. Though the author so far has experienced only a GT with the automatic, magazine road tests show 0 to 60 times of 6.7 to 6.9 seconds, a shade off an equivalent '93 model. With the automatic, it takes nearly 8 seconds to reach 60.

What is impressive are the great strides in handling that have been achieved over the previous generation Mustang. Whereas wheelspin was a matter of course if one tromped hard on the accelerator, especially if the roads had recently been rained upon, in the same conditions the latest Mustang stuck like glue. No waddle, no wiggle, no lashing side to side like an angry alligator. Part of the improvement can be attributed to suspension

TOP. *The 1994 Mustang handles as well as it looks, with great style.*

RIGHT AND ABOVE. *A cloth top is standard for the convertible but some might like the available fiberglass hardtop with full headlining. The traditional 1964 side scoop is back with the 1994 body which carries built-in spoilers and side-skirts.*

FAR RIGHT. *Beginning in 1964, again in 1979, Mustang scores with a third Indianapolis Pace Car in 1994. Here all three Pace Cars are assembled on the famous Brick Yard Oval.*

RIGHT. *Both coupe and convertible 1994 Mustangs are the most handsome since the first, 30 years before.*

modifications and huge 17-inch by 8-inch alloy wheels shod in 245/452R-17 tires. Standard wheels, incidentally, are 16 inches on the GT, 15 inches on the 6-cylinder powered car.

Certainly, the fourth-generation Mustang can hold its own against all-comers in fast cornering. Quick, positive rack and pinion steering guides the car through the bends with only a trace of understeer. And the standard 10.8-inch (front), 10.5-inch (rear) disk brakes coupled with optional ABS bring the car to a speedy and safe stop without fuss or bother.

Although the analog speedometer tracks to 150 mph, true top speed of the be-spoilered GT is around 138 to 140 mph; more than fast enough for America's speed-trapped super highways, where to go faster than 65 in a sporty car is inviting trouble of the most unwelcome kind. If you don't feel safe driving along a lonely western desert road at an unmentionable rate of knots, make sure you have an Escort radar detector for company.

On May 30, 1964, a Mustang first paced the classic Indianapolis 500 race. Fifteen years later, another Mustang paced Indy. And 30 years later, the fourth-generation Mustang paced the great race, this time a bright red Mustang Cobra convertible. Just 1,000 of these were produced and these were eagerly and quickly snapped up by buyers who had ordered them well before their release.

At Indianapolis in 1994, Parnelli Jones led the 33-car field to the start of the race. There were two more Cobras, one driven by another racing legend, driver A.J. Foyt, the other by Ford Chairman Alex Trotman. Trotman, if you recall, was Executive Vice President of Ford North American Operations and greatly encouraged the creation of the new Mustang. Promotion has been swift for Trotman, the first Briton to be chairman of America's second largest automobile corporation.

A product of Ford's Special Vehicle Team (SVT), the Cobra is no stranger to superior handling, speed, and roadability. The new model has all the others beat by a length. SVT engineers coaxed a further 25 horses out of the 5.0-liter V8 to give the Cobra 240 hp with 285 lbs/ft of torque at 4000 rpm. Top speed is about 150 mph, 0 to 60 in about 6 seconds.

And that, ladies and gentlemen, is that: three decades of Mustang to a rebirth of America's best-loved pony. The new Mustang is without doubt the best Mustang. . . and so it should be. It still hangs onto a rigid rear axle, but as Mike Zevalkink said, the ends don't yet justify the means. To develop a decent front engine, rear-drive car with all-independent suspension is to be thought about for the future. Considering the time and money that would have to be spent, the days of the standard Mustang costing $14,000 would be gone.

In the meantime, thanks to Skunkworks and Team Mustang, an American Legend will gallop into the 21st century and beyond.

The legendary pony graces the front of the fourth-generation Mustang, not that its namesake seems to have noticed! The 1994 car has styling which blends all themes into one attractive unit and the built-in spoilers work without the aggressive look of the previous generation.

9
RESTORATION AND THE ALTERNATIVE MUSTANG

There are two kinds of car enthusiast: the purist and the customizer. Yet maybe that's too general a description because there are so many variations on the two themes. Perhaps purist is a less complex term, because it sums up the car collector who buys a rotting hulk and meticulously restores it back to original, back to the way it looked the day it left the factory years before.

Customizer is really a term to describe people who chop and change, flatten and flame a dog-eared everyday car because its design lends itself to alternative styling. However, the customizer school of enthusiasts has branches such as the hot rodders, the funny-car builders, and the performance boys. At the end of the day, they can all be lumped together, for they are, in essence, pursuing the same goal: individuality, for availing themselves of self-expression, or to simply be noticed.

Many of the famous – and not so famous – automobile stylists started life customizing cars. Some were busy frenching headlights or adding fender skirts even in their teens. Once into adulthood, many of those not in Detroit set up shop on their own, men like George Barris, Gene Winfield, and Mad Daddy Roth, three famous California-based customizers who list film stars and film companies among their clients.

Once hot rodding was a young man's thing, the way to show you were the coolest cat in town. That was in the Fifties. Now hot rodders are family men with grown-up children, dreaming wistfully of days gone by, when *Peggy Sue* was top of the charts. One automobile and truck stylist comes particularly to mind.

He's well into his sixties now, but the fire of automotive creation still burns bright. He got himself a beat-up Datsun, painted it and lacquered it, beefed up the suspension, added a new rear end, and shoveled a big block Chevy V8 under the hood. It's a terrifying machine, yet it handles well and goes like no-tomorrow. So on hot summer nights, our ex-California friend tears up the Indiana lanes in this Chevy/Datsun dreaming of the good things, the good times. And why not?

What our hot-rodding friend has done is possibly something most of us would like to do, but haven't the knowledge to pull off. It's mostly our fear of what our friends and neighbors may think. Why worry? At least it shows that some of us are still alive in spirit and not downtrodden by events; our faces may be lined, but perpetual youth beats vibrantly in our hearts. Odds are you'll live longer, too.

LEFT AND ABOVE. Lee Iacocca created the Mustang as a car the buyer could build from the vast list of options, handling packages, and engines available. It was a car, somebody said, with a chameleon's ability to change from one personality to another. Over the years, owners took Iacocca literally and have done their own thing. Here is a mildly customized '65 fastback with a '66 grille, 1970 "Magnum" 500 wheels, racing-style hood pins, and a Shelby-like hood scoop. The overall effect is quite pleasing, and the car could be returned to original with ease.

MUSTANG AND ITS RESTORERS

So what is all this leading up to? Quite simply, the conflict between the purists and the customizer/hot rodder and how it has affected the Mustangs. Many dismiss those younger Mustang owners who take bits off, put things on, chrome suspension parts, and add fat slicks at the rear. The author doesn't pretend to be a follower of alternative cars, preferring originality. Nevertheless, some of these cars are recognizable art forms and should be accepted for what they are.

Detroit, of course, got wise to alternatives decades ago, especially in the Fifties when the motto was paint your car any color so long as it isn't black. Multicolored hues adorned those Fifties autos. It was also the start of the cult of the individual. In those days, a base car was exactly what it was; an engine, bodywork, transmission, and wheels. Little else. Then the salesman produced the options list. You could literally build your own car just the way you wanted it. The model range seemed never ending.

Take Chevrolet, for example. Their 110, 210, Delray, Biscayne and Bel-Air models were complete series in their own right. The 110 was the cheapest, the Bel-Air the most expensive. And you could spend as little or as much as you desired. It is a policy which still exists today. Most manufacturers offer a bewildering range of models.

Lee Iacocca thought like that, which is why the Mustang was touted as a car you could build yourself from the enormous array of available options. The basic car started at $2,363, but most people added a further $900 or $1,000 worth of options. A personal car it was meant to be, and a personal car it became.

There were almost 150 options and accessories to choose from in Mustang's first year, not counting eight models from three series. There was the Interior Decor group, the GT Equipment Group, Special Handling Package, the Visibility Group, Four different engines, each with its own high performance kit; 13- or 14-inch tires and wheels, tachometers and radios; all the extras needed to turn the buyer's Mustang into a plain-jane highway cruiser or a barn-storming powerhouse. The fact that the average customer spent around 25 percent extra on options confirms that the buyers desired to be different,

and as far as the car companies were concerned, their individualism meant healthy profits.

Today's youngsters are more conscious of their individuality than ever before. You only have to look around to see why. It's in the nature of things to be different, to stand out from the crowd so that the prettiest girl notices – and, hopefully, is impressed. Quite a lot of collectors with young families have restored their Mustangs back to 100 percent factory original, but there, in the corner of the garage is a Mach I complete with rubber-burning slicks, heightened rear end, and a wild paint job. He says it's his son's; his son says it started out that way, but all he ever gets to drive now is the Escort!

A lot of purists despair of what they consider sacrilege. Certainly to take a priceless Duesenberg, hack the body off, and replace it with a new one to the owner's taste would be sacrilege. The same rule applies to any great classic surviving in small numbers. There are, however, quite a few Duesenbergs running around with new bodies, the same with many a Rolls, Cadillac, or even Bugatti.

Customizers of these cars might argue that before the war the customer could choose what sort of body he wanted, so why not now? The answer is simple. What was built then was the norm, made from the then-current materials, which today creates a valid historical context. It should be pointed out, though, that to fabricate a replica body on a car salvaged from a pile of rotting metal,

woodwork, and brass is quite acceptable, the idea being to restore the car as well as possible to its original state.

Since 1964 there have been millions of Mustangs built, many of which are still running. Everybody loves them, so few are likely to end up in the crusher. Some, probably most, if they need restoring, will end up looking better than the day when they left the factory. Quite a few will be customized or given the performance treatment.

If it's a performance job, it's normally the under-thirties who opt for it. Growing up during the Mustang's heyday, most were too young to experience a full-blown Mustang in flight, let alone drive one. All they could do was to watch enviously as their elders burned rubber, worked on them, or just showed off in them. These youngsters might have been lucky and been given rides in a Mustang. One day, the kids dreamed, I'll have a car like this.

A lot changed over the ensuing 30 years: emissions, safety, lower speed limits. No more gut-wrenching muscle from the factories; instead, there followed the anemic era, a time not sympathetic to young, adventurous spirits.

BETTER, BUT MORE EXPENSIVE
Much has changed since 1979. Cars are better; they handle, go and stop well. Trouble is, they cost so much. A loaded Mustang or Camaro today would take the greater proportion of a young man's salary, perhaps even more depending on his job. What recourse has he but to

follow in the footsteps of enterprising generations before him and build performance himself.

Buying a used Mustang is easy; there are plenty around. A look through the local newspaper will probably find one. Failing that, there's the excellent *Hemming's Motor News*, a monthly with more than 1,000 pages of cars and related mobilia for sale every month with hundreds of Mustangs for sale, from $1,500 up. Reasonable cars, say 1964½-1966 models seem to average around $5,000. For the Mustang hunter, *Hemmings* is a good bet, the $4.95 cover price possibly turning out to be a blue chip investment in the long run.

Why the 1979–1993 cars? Quite simply, they lend themselves to the modifier's art, not only as individual one-off deals but as limited production vehicles as well. If you really want something loaded with power, improved handling, and striking looks, buy a Saleen or McLaren Mustang. Both companies are well established, have excellent relations with Ford, and build cars that will blow anything away in a traffic-light grand prix.

Nowadays, enthusiasts tend to leave 1964½ through 1973 Mustangs alone, or restore them to original stock condition. Instead, Mustangs built from 1979 to 1993 have become popular favorites for the modifier's skills. In fact, modifying third generation Mustangs has become big business, no longer the domain of the weekend builder. A large cottage industry has grown up with the express purpose of creating exciting alternative Mustangs.

Should an owner of one of the aforesaid Mustang models want his/her car given extra muscle, there are some very good places to go. Highly recommended are Chuck Watson of Detroit (313–946–9856), Charlie Bruno in San Jose (408–275–6511), and J. Bittle Associates of San Diego (619–560–2030).

To see the kind of modifications they do, buy America's hottest-selling Mustange magazine. Published by CSK, one of the top automotive publishing houses in the U.S.A., *Muscle Mustangs and Fast Fords* deals only with cars from 1979 on. Jim Campisano is the jocular, enthusiastic editor of a truely enterprising publication that has become the bible for late-model Mustang enthusiasts. Call CSK Publishing on 201–712–9300 for subscriptions or any other information you might need.

Though the purists might object – and there's no reason to, as they probably did the same in their youth – there is nothing wrong in what these youngsters are doing. It's healthy, beneficial, and a part of growing up. They learn a lot about mechanics, and some have gone on to bright careers in the auto industry. And as long as there are enough Mustangs to go around, what better way is there of spending a Saturday afternoon than creating a wholly personal car the way Lee Iacocca envisaged Mustang to be. As he said himself, the Mustang was to be a do-it-yourself car from the outset.

*THESE PAGES. **Some of the nasties awaiting the unsuspecting buyer: the dreaded rust attacks under the hood, shock towers, floor pan, near quarter panels, and trunk. The example shown, minus engine, is not actually too bad.***

The mean machine look. What a lot of young men – and older ones, too – do to achieve stable handling and more road grip. There's a 428 CJ in this '69.

THE WAY OF THE CUSTOMIZER

The customizer on the other hand is a different breed. He is only interested in the esthetic qualities of the car and whether he can embellish, remodel, and turn it into a work of motoring art. As mentioned earlier, some have made full-time careers out of customizing. Unlike the rodder's car, any Mustang that is heavily customized can rarely be returned to its original condition. An example turned up on the letters page of *Super Customs & Hot Rod* magazine. It had undergone a transformation that, in this writer's opinion, did nothing to improve upon the original. It had three inches shaved off the roof (a chopped top), lowered suspension, integral molded bumpers, skirts, front and rear modifications, and a landau effect on the roof's rear pillars. The work itself appeared well-executed, but as Mustangs go, it was a lost cause.

Late-Forties and Fifties cars lent themselves more readily to customizing due to their rounded shapes. The more angular lines of Sixties models do not, and as they are not as plentiful as they once were, it is to be hoped that customizers will leave them alone. If any period of Mustang would benefit from these artists' work, it would be late-model cars.

The purist is interested only in restoring the car to its original specifications, painting it in original factory colors and even going to great lengths to find original equipment tires. This, of course, is the right way to restore cars, the only way if a particular model is scarce. Fortunately, there are still enough Mustangs still around for restorers of all points of view to have a crack of the whip.

The collector can, if he or she chooses, pay more for a fully restored model culled from that excellent collectors' mart, the formerly mentioned *Hemmings Motor News*. Often good sources are *Old Cars Weekly* and *Cars and Parts*. Then, of course, there are *Auto Trader* and local newspaper classified ads.

Because the choice is large, it is best to shop around when trying to "corral" a Mustang, and follow a few simple rules. Never go to look at one at dusk; it's surprising how many sins the evening light can hide. And remember, too, that you're looking for cars that have long since lost the bloom of youth, so expect the worst. There is always going to be the "bondo special," cleverly but cheaply sprayed over to give it that "good original condition." Hopefully, the seller will point out his Mustang's faults because he is encouraged by the knowledge he'll sell it anyway, even if he has to take less for it.

Rust is a major problem on any car more than five years old unless it has been driven solely in southern California, parts of Arizona, Texas, New Mexico, Florida, and Georgia. Southern California is the only area likely to provide rust-free examples. This is fine for those who live close to the west coast, but generally speaking, the climate is pretty kind to cars driven west of Kansas. As we all know, it's in the North, Midwest and the East, in the states where salt is poured onto the roads to combat snow and ice in the winter months, that the ravages of rust take hold.

THESE PAGES. Another wild '69 sportsroof. Raised suspension, huge rear tires, and possibly traction bars will give better control in straight line take-offs. Sharp paint, sports slats, and spoilers are there for eye-grabbing effect.

THESE PAGES. Mustangs can be raced as well, not only by big professional teams, but by the boy next door as well. Here, ready for a race, is a 1970 Mustang run by a car dealership.

WHAT TO LOOK FOR

As a collector, once you have located a Mustang you consider suitable, go over it carefully for signs of tinworm. If the car looks freshly painted, it would be a good idea to run a strong magnet over the body. If there's metal under the lacquer, the magnet will stick; if it's bondo or plastic filler, the magnet will not adhere to the surface. A magnet is a very useful detector and can save a lot of trouble and expense.

Mustangs from 1964½ to 1973 have built-in rust problems which always manifest themselves in the same areas of the body: the floorpan, front and rear, bottom edges of the doors, inner wheelhouse, outer quarter panel, rear quarter panels, the trunk floor where it is attached to the frame rail, and the curl around the air vent below the windshield. Convertibles have additional rust traps, chiefly where extra reinforcing for the understructure begins to go. Once the rust has taken hold in these areas, the convertible will start sagging in the middle.

By the nature of its design, the Mustang has a habit of rusting out under the hood. Front fender aprons can be a real problem, as can the shock tower. Once rust has taken hold, it rots everything from cowl to radiator support. On convertibles, the inner rocker panel and torque box are very prone to deterioration.

If you have a Mustang with these problems, you may well have a few mechanical ones as well. Early three-speed manual transmissions are a real headache and are best avoided. Ford engines, though, are pretty reliable, and there should be little trouble with these, especially the six and the 289s. Still, it would be advisable to check for oil leaks. Start the engine up and take the car for a short drive up the road. A 10-minute run should confirm to you whether the Mustang is mechanically sound.

Fortunately, a scruffy Mustang doesn't have to be given the coup de grace; the writer has seen cars rescued from the depths of despair and renovated to become show-class winners. Ford can still provide 90 percent of body and mechanical parts for Mustangs as far back as 1964½. If Ford is unable to satisfy you, there are numerous companies who supply a wide range of perfect reproduction parts from screws to upholstery. As for part prices, there seems little variation between the companies, who all provide the same service. As the part numbers seem to be the same, it is worth shopping around if a lot of items are needed.

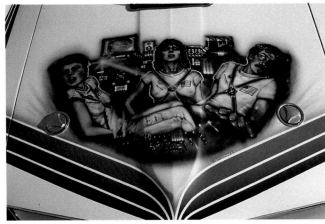

*ABOVE, RIGHT AND OPPOSITE PAGE. **Some customizers go too far, but here is a well-conceived, beautifully rendered mild custom. Attention to detail and the painted mural reveal artistic talent.***

FINDING SPARES

Where do you go for Mustang spares? Try Ford dealerships first, then the Mustang specialists who seem to be popping up in ever-increasing numbers. Three of the well-established companies are: Dallas Mustang Parts, 9515 Skillman, Dallas, Texas 75243. Toll-free number: 1-800-527-1223 outside Texas. In state: 1-800-442-1047. Information: 1-214-349-0091. Larry's Thunderbird & Mustang Parts, Inc., 511 S. Raymond Ave., Fullerton, California 92631. Phone toll-free: 1-800-854-0393. California Mustang, 1249 E. Holt, Dept. C G, Pomona, California 91767. Phone: 1-714-623-6551. Toll-free order number 1-800-854-1737. At the time of going to press all these companies appear to have Visa/Mastercard facilities.

On the face of it, the quality of spares from these suppliers seems first class, but it is always worth checking with someone first, like another Mustang owner/collector or friend who may have had some dealings previous with them.

Another source of assistance is the clubs. The national organization is the Mustang Club of America, which is well worth joining. It has chapters all over the United States, and there are independent clubs affiliated with it. One is the Old Fort Mustangers of Fort Wayne, Indiana. This club, to which the writer proudly belongs, holds splendid rallies, organizes fund-raising for charity, and owns some of the finest Mustangs in the Midwest — as can be seen in the pages of this book. It was its members' help, advice, and inspiration that enabled this book

to be written.

If you wish to restore a Mustang, it is necessary to know what you are doing. Dobbs Publications Inc., of Lakeland, Florida, publishers of the fine *Mustang Monthly* magazine, has put out a series of books on the subject. One, the *Mustang Recognition Guide 1964½–1973* is the Mustang bible. It contains everything the aspiring Mustang owner needs to know, because it is a year-by-year analysis of all models, accessories, engines, and trim, etc. Having studied and accumulated the knowledge this great work imparts, you should be able to look at a door panel and say what year it came from. Copiously illustrated, it is the Mustang book to buy.

Besides the recognition guide, Mustang Publications also issues a series of year-by-year fact books about the 1965 to 1973 models. Each book is a comprehensive guide to the year in question. Then there's a series of how-to books, from engine re-builds to re-spraying; all necessary for the true Mustang connoisseur.

Mustang. Who would have thought this inexpensive little car would have generated as much love and interest as it did? It was certainly the right car at the right time, born of an inspired hunch of an Italian-American called Lee Iacocca. Whatever its shortcomings (and it had them), the Mustang galloped its way into America's, and the world's, heart and automotive history. There is only one other car that universally matches it in mystique, and that car is Ferrari. Yet the Ferrari is a European thoroughbred, virtually handbuilt and costing several times as much, while Mustangs were stamped out in their hundreds of thousands.

Like Ferrari, the Mustang is universally accepted and recognized. The Mustang Club of Great Britain, for example, has almost 1,000 members; large clubs devoted to its memory proliferate in Europe while in Australia, Mustangs are the cars to have. The secret of its success lies in its earthy, good looks (1964½–1969), even temperament (if blessed with a 289), and youthful appeal. However old and wearied, one feels young again with the magic the Mustang creates. It may not be a pampered thoroughbred or a blueblood, but with its honesty and popular appeal, the Mustang struck a chord with the world.

In Mustang, the market finally found its car.

APPENDIX

MUSTANG
SPECIFICATIONS

SPECIFICATIONS 1964½–65

Body type	Sales 1964½ – 65
Hardtop	456,747
Convertible	93,712
Fastback 3-door	68,784
TOTAL SALES	619,243

Models	Price/Weights (lbs)
Hardtop, 6	$2,372/2,445
Hardtop, 8	$2,480/2,720
Convert, 6	$2,614/2,669
Convert, 8	$2,722/2,904
Fastback, 6	$2,589/2,495
Fastback, 8	$2,697/2,770

General Specifications (inches)	1964½	1965
Wheelbase	108.0	180.0
Overall length	181.6	181.6
Overall width	68.2	68.2
Standard Trans.	3-speed manual	3-speed manual
Optional Trans.	Overdrive 4-speed manual 3-speed automatic	Overdrive 4-speed manual 3-speed automatic

Engine Availability Type	CID	HP	1964½	1965
I-6	170	101	Standard	—
I-6	200	120	—	Standard
V8	260	164	Standard	—
V8	289	200	Optional	Standard
V8	289	225	Optional	Optional
V8	289	271	Optional	Optional

SPECIFICATIONS 1966–68

Body type	1966	1967	Sales 1968
Hardtop	450,352	334,059	235,031
Convertible	64,990	42,014	23,910
Fastback 3-door	32,169	66,613	40,120
TOTAL SALES	547,511	442,686	299, 061

Models	1966	Price/Weights (lbs) 1967	1968
Hardtop, 6	$2,416/2,488	$2,461/2,568	$2,602/2,635
Convert, 6	$2,653/2,650	$2,698/2,738	$2,814/2,745
Fastbck, 6	$2,607/2,519	$2,592/2,605	$2,712/2,659

General Specifications (inches)	1966	1967	1968
Wheelbase	108.0	108.0	180.0
Overall length	181.6	183.6	183.6
Overall width	68.2	70.9	70.9
Standard Trans.	3-speed manual	3-speed manual	3-speed manual
Optional Trans.	4-speed manual 3-speed automatic	4-speed manual 3-speed automatic	4-speed manual 3-speed automatic

Engine Availability Type	CID	HP	1966	1967	1968
I-6	200	120	Standard	Standard	—
I-6	200	115	—	—	Standard
V8	289	195/200	Optional	Optional	Optional
V8	289	225	Optional	Optional	—
V8	289	271	Optional	Optional	—
V8	302	230	—	—	Optional
V8	390	320/325	—	Optional	Optional
V8	427	390	—	—	Optional

SPECIFICATIONS 1969–70

Body type	1969	Sales 1970
Hardtop	147,381	85,703
Convertible	14,427	6,839
Fastback 3-door	131,530	77,461
TOTAL SALES	293,338	170,003

Models	Price/Weights (lbs) 1969	1970
Hardtop, 6	$2,635/2,690	$2,721/2,721
Fastback, 6	$2,635/2,713	$2,771/2,745
Convert, 6	$2,849/2,800	$3,025/2,831
Grandé, 8	$2,866/2,765	$2,936/2,806
Hardtop, V8	$2,740/2,906	$2,822/2,923
Fastback, V8	$2,740/2,930	$2,872/2,947
Boss 302, V8	$3,588/3,210	$3,720/3,227
Convert, V8	$2,954/3,016	$3,126/3,033
Grandé, V8	$2,971/2,981	$3,028/3,008
Mach I, V8	$3,139/3,175	$3,371/3,240

General Specifications (inches)	1969	1970
Wheelbase	108.0	180.0
Overall length	187.4	187.4
Overall width	71.3	71.7
Standard Trans.	3-speed manual	3-speed manual
Optional Trans.	4-speed manual 3-speed automatic	4-speed manual 3-speed automatic

Engine Availability Type	CID	HP	1969	1970
I-6	200	115/120	Standard	Standard
I-6	250	155	Optional	Optional
V8	302	220	Standard[a]	Standard[a]
V8	351	250	Optional[b]	Optional[b]
V8	351	290/300	Optional	Optional
V8	390	320	Optional	—
V8	428	335	Optional	Optional
V8	428[c]	335	Optional	Optional
V8	429[d]	375	Optional	Optional

a: 290 hp std Boss 302   b: Std. Mach 1   c: with Ram Air   d: Boss 429

SPECIFICATIONS 1971–73

Body type	1971	1972	Sales 1973
Hardtop	77,697	72,277	70,229
Convertible	5,723	6,136	10,845
Fastback 3-door	56,523	41,507	42,327
TOTAL SALES	139,943	119,920	123,401

Models	Price/Weights (lbs) 1971	1972	1973
Hardtop, 6	$2,911/2,937	$2,729/2,941	$2,760/2,995
Fastback, 6	$2,973/2,907	$2,786/2,908	$2,820/2,008
Convert, 6	$3,227/3,059	$3,015/3,051	$3,102/3,126
Grandé, 6	$3,117/2,963	$2,915/2,965	$2,946/3,003
Hardtop, V8	$3,006/3,026	$2,816/3,025	$2,897/3,085
Fastback, V8	$3,068/2,993	$2,873/2,995	$2,907/3,098
Boss 302, V8	$4,124/3,281	—	—
Convert, V8	$3,320/3,145	$3,101/3,147	$3,189/3,216
Grandé, V8	$3,212/3,049	$3,002/3,051	$3,088/3,115
Mach I, V8	$3,268/3,220	$3,053/3,046	$3,088/3,115

General Specifications (inches)	1971	1972	1973
Wheelbase	109.0	109.0	109.0
Overall length	187.5(6) 189.5(8)	— 190.0	— 194.0
Overall width	75.0	75.0	75.0
Standard Trans.	3-speed manual	3-speed manual	3-speed manual
Optional Trans.	4-speed manual	4-speed manual	4-speed manual
	3-speed automatic	3-speed automatic	3-speed automatic

Engine Availability Type	CID	HP	1971	1972	1973
I-6	250	145 (gross)[a]	Standard	Standard	Standard
V8	302	210 (gross)[b]	Standard	Standard	Standard
V8	351	240 (gross)	Optional	—	—
V8	351	285 (gross)	Optional	—	—
V8	351	280 (gross)	Optional	—	—
V8	351	330 (gross)	Standard[c]	—	—
V8	429	370 (gross)	Optional	—	—
V8	351	168 (net)	—	Optional	Optional
V8	351	200 (net)	—	Optional	Optional
V8	351	275 (net)	—	Optional	—

a: rated 95hp (net) 1972-3   b: rated 136hp (net) 1972-73   c: Std. Boss 351 only

SPECIFICATIONS
1974–78

Body type	1974	1975	1976	1977	Sales 1978
Hardtop	204,892	145,220	110,440	102,680	107,971
Convertible	0	0	0	0	0
Fastback 3-door	91,149	53,979	68,101	58,974	71,068
TOTAL SALES	296,041	199,199	178,541	161,654	179,039

Models	1974	1975	Price/Weights (lbs) 1976	1977	1978
2-door, 4	$3,134/2,620	$3,529/2,660	$3,525/3,678	$3,702/2,627	$3,731/2,608
3-door, 4	$3,328/2,699	$3,818/2,697	$3,781/2,706	$3,901/2,672	$3,975/2,654
Ghia 2-door, 4	$3,480/2,886	$3,939/2,704	$3,859/2,729	$4,119/2,667	$4,149/2,646
2-door, V-6	$3,363/2,689	$3,801/2,775	$3,791/2,756	$3,984/2,750	$3,944/2,705
3-door, V-8	$3,557/2,768	$4,210/2,812	$4,047/2,784	$4,183/2,795	$4,188/2,751
Ghia 2-door, V-6	$3,709/2,755	$2,873/2,819	$4,125/2,807	$4,401/2,790	$4,362/2,743
Mach I, V6	$3,674/2,778	$2,911/2,879	$4,209/2,822	$4,332/2,046	$4,430/2,733

General Specifications (inches)	1974	1975	1976	1977	1978
Wheelbase	96.2	96.2	96.2	96.2	96.2
Overall length	175.0	175.0	175.0	175.0	175.0
Overall width	70.2	70.2	70.2	70.2	70.2
Standard Trans.	4-speed manual	4-speed manual	4-speed manual	4-speed manual	4-speed manual
Optional Trans.	3-speed automatic	3-speed automatic	3-speed automatic	3-speed automatic	3-speed automatic

Engine Availability Type	CID	HP	1974	1975	1976	1977	1978
I-4	140	a	Standard	Standard	Standard	Standard	Standard
V8	171	b	Optionald	Optional	Optional	Optional	Optional
V8	302	c	—	Optional	Optional	Optional	Optional

a: rated 85hp 1974; 83hp 1975; 92hp 1976; 89hp 1977; 88hp 1978   c: rated 122hp 1975; 139hp 1976-78
b: rated 105hp 1974; 97hp 1975; 103 1976; 93hp 1977; 90hp 1978   d: Standard Mach I

SPECIFICATIONS
1979–80

Body type	1979	Sales 1980
Hardtop	188,150	123,435
Convertible	0	0
Fastback 3-door	114,159	122,573
TOTAL SALES	302,309	246,008

1979 Models	Price/Weights (lbs)
Base 2-door	$4,494/2,530
Base 3-door	$4,828/2,612
Ghia 2-door	$5,064/2,648
Ghia 3-door	$5,216/2,672

1980 Models	Price/Weights (lbs)
Base 2-door	$4,884/2,606
Base 3-door	$5,194/2,614
Ghia 2-door	$5,369/NA
Ghia 3-door	$5,512/NA

General Specifications (inches)	1979	1980
Wheelbase	100.4	100.4
Overall length	179.1	179.1
Overall width	69.1	69.1
Standard Trans.	4-speed manual (4 cyl.) 4-speed manual w/overdrive (V6 and V8)	4-speed manual (4 cyl.) 4-speed manual (6 cyl.) 3-speed automatic (8 cyl.)
Optional Trans.	3-speed automatic	3-speed automatic

Engine Availability Type	CID	HP	1979	1980
I-4	140	88	Standard	Standard
Turbo-4	140	131	Optional	Optional
I-6	200	85	Optional	Optional
V8	255	117	Optional	Optional

SALES 1981–85

Body type	1981	1982	1983	1984	Sales 1985
Hardtop	88,838	46,159	31,299	35,092	59,122
Convertible	0	0	23,620	16,950	16,182
Fastback 3-door	84,491	70,645	61,202	79,719	84,437
TOTAL SALES	179,329	116,804	116,121	131,761	159,741

SPECIFICATIONS 1986–88

Body type	1986	1987	Sales 1988
Hardtop	67,456	44,085	38,291
Convertible	19,550	23,599	26,838
Fastback 3-door	88,592	95,708	105,472
TOTAL SALES	175,598	163,392	170,601

Models		Price/Weights (lbs)	
	1986	1987	1988
LX 2-door cpe.	$7,295	$8,043/2,724	$8,835/2,724
LX 3-door cpe.	$7,807	$8,474/2,782	$9,341/2,782
LX 2-door conv.	$12,677	$12,840/3,214	$13,702/3,214
GT 3-door cpe.	$10,567	$11,835/2,782	$12,745/2,782
GT 2-door conv.	$14,420	$15,724/3,214	16,610/3,214
SVO 2-door cpe.	$15,286	—	—

General Specifications (inches)	1986	1987	1988
Wheelbase	100.5	100.5	100.5
Overall length	179.3	179.6	179.6
Overall width	69.1	69.1	69.1
Standard Trans.	4-speed manual	4-speed manual	4-speed manual
Optional Trans.	3-speed automatic	4-speed automatic	4-speed automatic

Engine Availability Type	CID (liters)	HP	1986	1987	1988
OHC I-4	140 (2.3)	90	Standard	Standard	Standard
OHV V8	302 (4.9)	225	Standard w/GT	Standard w/GT	Standard w/GT

SPECIFICATIONS 1989–91

Body type	1989	1990	Sales 1991
Hardtop	31,847	18,611	16,876
Convertible	35,309	26,708	20,143
Fastback 3-door	105,062	75,168	53,441
TOTAL SALES	172,218	120,487	90,460

Models		Price/Weights (lbs)	
	1989	1990	1991
LX 2-door notchback	$9,050/2,754	$9,456/2,759	$10,157/2,759
LX 3-door hatchback	$9,556/2,819	$9,962/2,824	$10,663/2,824
LX 2-door conv.	$14,140/2,966	$15,141/2,960	$16,222/2,960
LX 5.0L Sport 2-door notchback	$11,410/2,754	$12,164/2,759	$13,270/2,759
LX 5.0L Sport 3-door hatchback	$12,265/2,819	$13,007/2,824	$14,055/2,824
LX 5.0L Sport 2-door. conv.	$17,001/2,966	$18,183/2,960	$19,242/2,960
GT 3-door hatch.	$13,272/2,819	$13,986/2,824	$15,034/2,824
GT 2-door conv.	$17,512/2,966	$18,805/2,960	$19,864/2,960

General Specifications (inches)	1989	1990	1991
Wheelbase	100.5	100.5	100.5
Overall length	179.6	179.6	179.6
Overall width	69.1	68.3	68.3
Standard Trans.	5 speed manual	5 speed manual	5 speed manual
Optional Trans.	4 speed automatic	4 speed automatic	4 speed automatic

Engine Availability Type	CID (liters)	HP	1989	1990	1991
OHC I-4	140 (2.3)	88	Standard	—	—
OHC I-4	140 (2.3)	105	—	Standard	Standard
OHV V8	302 (5.0)	325	Standard w/GT	Standard w/GT	Standard w/GT

SPECIFICATIONS
1992–94

Body type	1992	1993	Sales 1994
Hardtop	13,428	20,127	91,300 (est.)
Convertible	22,235	24,063	0
Fastback 3-door	24,063	52,035	45,700 (est.)
TOTAL SALES	71,904	96,225	137,000 (est.)

Models	Price/Weights (lbs)		
	1992	1993	1994
LX 2.3L 2-door cpe.	$10,215/2,775	$10,215/2,775	
Mustang 2-door cpe.			$13,365/3,055
Mustang 2-door conv.			$20,160/3,255
LX 2.3L 3-door cpe.	$10,721/2,834	$10,721/2,834	
LX 2.3L conv.	$16,899/2,996	$16,899/2.996	
LX 5.0L 2-door cpe	$13,422	$13,422	
LX 5.0L 3-door cpe	$14,207	$14,207	
LX 5.0L conv.	$19,644	$19,644	
GT 5.0L 3-door cpe.	$15,243	$15,243	
GT 5.0L conv.	$20,199	$20,199	
Mustang GT cpe.			$17,280
Mustang GT conv.			$21,970
Cobra 3-door cpe.			—
1992 and 1993 were basically the same with weight, pricing and specifications			

General Specifications (inches)	1992	1993	1994
Wheelbase	100.5	100.5	100.3
Overall length	179.6	179.6	181.5
Overall width	68.3	68.3	71.8
Standard Trans.	5-speed manual	5-speed manual	5-speed manual
Optional Trans.	4-speed automatic	4-speed automatic	4-speed automatic

Engine Availability Type	CID (liters)	HP	1992	1993	1994
OHC I-4	140 (2.3)	105	Standard LX	Standard LX	—
OHV V6	232 (3.8)	145	—	—	Standard
OHV V8	302 (4.9)	205	Standard w/LX 5.0L	Standard w/LX 5.0L	—
OHV V8	302 (4.9)	215	—	—	Standard
OHV V8	302 (4.9)	245	Standard w/Cobra	Standard w/Cobra	—

INDEX

U.S. President Bill Clinton at the Mustang's 30th Anniversary celebrations. With him, from left, are: Bill Dillard, President of the Mustang Club of America; Bruton Smith, owner of the Charlotte Speedway where the event was held; and Alex Trotman, Ford Chief Executive Officer.

ACKNOWLEDGEMENTS

Nicky Wright gratefully acknowledges the following for their kind assistance and advice in making this book possible:

In the USA
Tom and Karen Barnes; Mike Barron and Luis Corona; Dennis, Christine and Donna Begley; Tom Bergman; Don and Judy Bergman; Tammy Burniston; Mike and Cathy Butler; Rod Butler; Phil Carpenter; Jim and Vickie Champion; Galen Chapman; Wayne Coffman; Bob and Elaine Cox; Stan Drall, Ford Motor Company; Mark Dollier; Auburn-Cord-Duesenberg Museum, Auburn, Ind; Chuck Edwards; Michael Erpenbach; Allen County Ford, Fort Wayne Ind; Noah Yoder Ford, Hicksville, Ohio; Harold and Darlene Glaves; Elton W. Gingerich; Wellard and Norma Hadley; Jeffrey A. Hamilton; Biff and Donna Hitzeman; Howard, Glen, Don, Wayne and all at Dobbs; Paul Ingram; David Jacoby; Steve and Rita Kemerly; Lonnie Krag, Copperstate Mustang Club, Phoenix, Arizona; Gerald and Michelle King; Mark London, Ford Motor Company; Jim Linnemeier; Skip and Kathy Marketti; Fred McHugh; Ronald, Robbie, Renea and Rick Miller—a special thank-you; Mrs Naomi Myers; Old Fort Mustangers, Fort Wayne, Ind; Ivan and Anna Penich; Carol and Tom Podemski; Bill and Jenny Pogue; Richard Pogue; Rick Purdy; Jack, Ruth, Kari, Kim and Snoopy Randinelli; Ron Remke; Craig and Clay Sanderson; Sanderson Auto Sales, South Main, Auburn, Ind; Ed Sawtell, Ford PR, Ford Motor Company; Jim and Ginger Schoenherr; Noah and Joyce Yoder; Unique Color Lab, Film Processors, Wells St, Fort Wayne, Ind; Kelly Watson; Walt and Marilyn Wise; Steve Yanner; Paul Zazarine; Mike Zevalkink, Ford Motor Company; also Fuji Films, Pentax and Nikon cameras with which all the photographs in this book were taken.

In the UK
Angie Arnold; Roy Hopkins; Barry Sturgess; Steve Turland; Mustang Club of Great Britain; Langley Colour Lab, Film Processors, Langley St., London (a special thanks to Arthur and Tom).

BIBLIOGRAPHY

Iacocca. An Autobiography. Lee Iacocca. Bantam Books, New York.

The Ford Mustang—1964–1973. Jerry Heasley. Tab Books, New York.

The Production Figure Book for US Cars. Jerry Heasley. Motorbooks International.

Mustang: The Original Ponycar. Consumer Guide, Skokie, Ill.

The Consumer Guide *Auto Test* Publications, 1974 to 1994.

1964½–1973 Mustang Recongnition Guide. Dobbs Publications Inc., Lakeland, Fla.

Shelby-American Guide. Rik Kopec. Shelby-American Club Publications.

Ford Mustang 1964–1967; Ford Mustang 1967–1973; Mustang Musclecars 1967–1971; Shelby Mustang Musclecars 1965–70. All published by Brooklands Books.

Motor Trend, Car & Driver, Road & Track, Muscle Mustangs & Fast Fords, and *Automobile* magazines.